To: Luby, Denise, and Delaney

YOU ARE HERE

May all your moments be joyful.

Sincerely,

Dora.

YOU ARE HERE

How to awaken your potential and live your greatest life <u>now</u>!

Dora Nudelman

MILL CITY PRESS

Copyright © 2012 by Dora Nudelman.

Mill City Press, Inc.
212 3rd Avenue North, Suite 290
Minneapolis, MN 55401
612.455.2294
www.millcitypublishing.com
All rights reserved. No part of this publication may be reproduced, stored in a retrieval system, or transmitted, in any form or by any means, electronic, mechanical, photocopying, recording, or otherwise, without the prior written permission of the author.

ISBN-13: 978-1-937600-48-8
LCCN: 2011943054

Cover Design and Typeset by Steve Porter

Printed in the United States of America

Acknowledgments

Thank you mom and dad for your continued love and support. Thank you from the bottom of my heart. I share this and all of my accomplishments with you. Thank you to all those who have had the courage and foresight to speak their truth, and as such, encourage, inspire, and uplift others to do the same. Thank you to all the great self-empowerment authors who have inspired me over the years through their wonderful and honest teachings, and who have unknowingly encouraged me to share my own truth. Thank you to all the wonderful teachers who have guided me along my journey, and to the great intuitive guides who continue to help me along my way. Thank you to all those who have supported me in pursuing my passions, and all those who have openly received and continue to receive that which I have to share. Thank you for supporting me with this platform. And of course, thank you to you, the reader, for being open and receptive to my words and for taking the time to receive the message I have to share with you. You are here reading this book for a reason, so I hope it awakens you to the answers you seek, I hope it brings you the courage you need to live your truth, and I hope it motivates you to take your life to the next level of total love, joy, peace, and true fulfillment, right now and in every moment.

Contents

Introduction	ix
Understanding Concepts	xiii
Chapter 1: What is Presence?	1
Chapter 2: Taking a Time-Out	9
Chapter 3: One with Nature	15
Chapter 4: Slowing Down	19
Chapter 5: Being Present in the Face of Technology	29
Chapter 6: Contemplation and Awareness	37
Chapter 7: Stillness	45
Chapter 8: Enjoying the Moment	51
Chapter 9: The Journey is the Goal	59
Chapter 10: Letting Go	65
Chapter 11: Acceptance and Allowing	79
Chapter 12: Releasing Fear and Dumping Regret	91
Chapter 13: Appreciation	115
Chapter 14: Detachment from the Outcome	121
Chapter 15: Fully Engaged	135
Chapter 16: Taking Inspired Action	141
Chapter 17: Releasing Negative Judgments	155
Chapter 18: You Have Already Arrived	165
Chapter 19: Observing the Observer	169
Chapter 20: Simplifying	179
Chapter 21: Planning for the Future	187
Chapter 22: Being in the Flow and Fulfilling Your Desires	199
Chapter 23: Being in the Flow and Creating Alignment	213
Chapter 24: Being in the Flow and Fulfilling Your Purpose	225
Chapter 25: No Limits	233
Epilogue	239
About the Author	241

Introduction

For some life is blissful. For others life is stressful. Ever wonder why that is? Why do some people feel fulfilled while others feel despaired? Why do some people enjoy their lives while others never seem to be satisfied? Is it related to money? Is it related to success? What is the deciding factor that takes a person from stress to bliss?

Let's look at time. Time has become even more of a commodity these days. As a result, we have come up with all sorts of so-called time-saving practices to help us manage our time well and to hopefully give us more of it. You would think, then, that we would actually have more time to spare and enjoy. Unfortunately, it seems as though we've completely missed the mark. We may have created more time for ourselves, but many of us have also ended up filling it up with stuff we really don't need. We've simply forgotten how to just be.

So perhaps the answer to the aforementioned question is that those who feel blissful are merely those who know how to make and spend their time well. Perhaps the secret to a happy life is as simple as being present in time rather than chasing after it.

We live in a world where running around frantically in an effort to get things done is not only understood, it's encouraged. We are constantly running from place to place and from task to task, but no matter where we go or what we do it just never feels good enough. There's always something more to do, somewhere else to go.

While there is nothing wrong with wanting to expand and grow, it's important that you don't take for granted where you are right now. The fact of the matter is that you are always here. No matter what you are doing, it's always happening right here, right now. While your mind may wander, you are never truly anywhere else but here.

You Are Here

Because now is the only real moment that ever exists, it's important that you understand what it truly means to live in the present moment. As individuals we have been giving more and more of our personal power away. We have become lost in regrets and fears, and as such, we've forgotten our true inherent nature that is Infinite Love, Happiness, and Total Abundance. As a society we have become less and less aware of our true purpose, which is to connect and share, to love and express. We have forgotten that we are all connected, and as a result, we've ended up living in an ego-dominated world of competition, dissatisfaction, and stress.

What we need to do is re-awaken ourselves to the truth of who we are at our core. We need to understand that we are constantly creating our future through what we are feeling, thinking, believing, and doing in each of our present moments. We need to remind ourselves that we have the power to make significant positive changes in our own lives, as well as influence others to do the same.

It's simple. Remembering our true power causes us to be empowered, and our true power always lies in the present moment. When we are freed through the present moment we no longer live in fear or regret. As a result, we no longer set limits for ourselves, nor do we sabotage our lives through insecurity and doubt. Instead, we become enlightened by knowing our truth and by being consciousness of that truth in relation to all that we do, all that we have, and all that we are.

To counteract the stress, struggle, confusion, or any degree of general dissatisfaction you may be experiencing in your life today, this book has been designed to help you realize your true power, and to show you how to use it to create the happiness you deserve.

The premise of this book is simple: it is to help you become aware of the most powerful moment you will ever have to create the life you want to live. And that moment is now. By recognizing the power within you right now, and by being fully engaged with it, you will not only become more conscious of your creative energy, you will also naturally release unwanted conditions from your life. You will truly know how to live a full and happy life, now and always.

Introduction

Consider this book as a tool to awaken you to what you already know within. Let it help you become conscious to all the blessings and opportunities in your life right now. Let it teach you how to feel fulfilled and peaceful within every moment. Then, if you are open to it, you will come into a new type of awareness and appreciation for life that will translate into the life you've always wanted to live.

Understanding Concepts

Throughout the pages of this book you will come across several major concepts that are discussed and utilized in helping to explain presence. As such, it is important at this time that some of these main concepts be clarified with respect to the context in which they are being presented here.

Energy:

Throughout this book you will see terms used such as Source Energy, Divine Intelligence, The Universe, and the like. Please view these terms as neutral descriptions of the vast energy from which all emanates. There are no religious or dogmatic connotations intended here whatsoever. It is for you to decide what these terms mean to you and interpret them in a way that resonates with you the most.

These terms are used for illustrative purposes only, because in truth, there really isn't one term that can properly or completely define that which is indefinable. Just know that whatever IT is, you are one with it, as is everyone and everything else.

Ego:

Ego is another term mentioned quite a bit in this book, so it's an important term to clarify. It's important for you to understand the role your ego plays in your life, and the context in which it is being presented here.

Nothing is really good or bad until we attach meaning to it. The ego can be seen in the same way. Some wonder why we have an ego to begin with. Why not just come here already being aware of our Divine Nature and eliminate all the pain and suffering caused by the ego in the first place?

We have to understand that the ego serves an important purpose in our evolution and in our development. While it can certainly cause chaos in our lives, it does so only when we let it get out of control.

We are spiritual beings having a physical experience. As such, we have physical as well as spiritual aspects to us. What the ego does is distinguish us from one another here on this physical plane. This is important because through our individualization we are driven to fulfill our unique purpose, express our personal talents and gifts, and share what we have with the world. Yes, we are all one and energetically connected, but we must also consider that each of us is an individualized expression of the whole.

We exist simultaneously in the physical dimension as well as in the spiritual (energetic) realm. As such, we are separate from one another (in appearance), yet one with each other (beneath the surface). We are all made of the same raw materials, but physically, emotionally, and mentally each of us is made up of a combination of things that results in our different appearances, relationships, perceptions, experiences, and other manifestations.

So yes, the ego can make us feel separate from one another, but how we interpret that separateness is up to us; will it be a feeling of lack and competition that we buy into, or will we use our individuality as a motivator to come into our full potential and share our unique expressions with the whole?

It is here on this physical plane that our separateness and our ensuing unique perspectives are free to become expressed. On the flip side, it is our knowledge of our oneness that allows us to use our free will to fully come into our true potential for the benefit of all. So, we can either choose to identify with the "me versus you" or "us versus them" mentality, which is a negative aspect of the ego. Or, we can choose to identify with our unique attributes as part of the whole, and as such, share our true selves with the world.

We are dynamic beings with many layers and intricacies. Subsequently, we can consider our egos as simply one element in the cocktail that makes up who we are. How we use it, however, is a personal choice. We can use it to feed into our insecurities and fears, or we can use it to our advantage to help us be more purposeful and sharing in our lives. The choice is ours. In fact, the ego only becomes troublesome when it takes over our lives and all of our choices. But if we as our true selves remain at the helm, our egos must then follow our instruction.

You are an individualized expression of the whole. We all are. And the ego is simply a part of that individuality on the physical level. Use that individuality to better understand yourself and what you are here to do, be, and have, and then acknowledge your oneness with everything else so that you can share your individuality with others in a way that is most beneficial for all.

Realize that the problem isn't in thinking of yourself as separate. The problem lies in only thinking of yourself as separate. So you must embrace the duality of your nature in order to fully appreciate your full potential. In truth, nothing is given to us without a purpose, so the ego must be included in that rationale. See your ego as neutral and malleable rather than as an evil part of yourself that you must completely eradicate. Know that evil comes from choice. The ego in and of itself is not bad. It's what you do with it that determines its nature and the consequences that ensue.

Often in talks about spirituality the ego is referred to as something that needs to be removed completely. But maybe it would be wiser to shift our focus onto controlling it rather than eliminating it, that way we'll be able to understand the boundaries of our physical separation, while also knowing that beneath it all we're all truly one.

So in the context of this book the ego is often referred to in relation to its negative aspects. However, as a general practice, think of the ego as something not to be totally eradicated, but rather as something to be tamed and transformed. Think of it as a driving force that helps you come into your true and full potential through the expression of your purpose and authentic passions. Then as you read about the ego from chapter to chapter, keep in mind that you have a choice, to let your ego control you, or to be in charge of it. Question where in your life you have allowed it to take over, and then use the guidance you receive here to transform any negative aspects of your ego into positive motivation instead.

Perfection:

You will also find the concept of "perfection" referred to quite a bit in this book. As such, it is important to clarify what perfection truly means in the context being used here.

True perfection is not some general standard you use to pressure yourself. It is not something you'll find on the cover of magazines or in your bank account. It cannot just be measured by your appearance, your job, your relationships, your savings, your investments, or anything else that's surface-level or external to you.

Perfection is something that is left to you to figure out for yourself. It is simply a state in which you feel whole and complete and at peace with yourself, right in each moment. Perfection is a term that describes the whole of you, blunders and all. It is the person you are meant to be, it is the truth you are meant to embody. Perfection is who you are at your core, no matter what. You are made of perfection and you are here to express your unique perfection. No one can tell you how to be perfect or what it will mean to you. You are here to decide for yourself and to choose a meaning that corresponds with truth and purpose rather than anything artificial or superficial.

If your concept of perfection is stressing you out, then perhaps it's time to re-evaluate where your definition is coming from. You are not here to pressure yourself into meeting someone else's standards. You are not here to impose harsh criticisms on yourself. You are here to be you, and to be the best you that you can be. That is where your personal perfection lies; in your mistakes, in your achievements, in your lessons, and in your expressions.

Perfect timing and perfect order, as mentioned throughout this book, then, are simply expressions of your purpose. They indicate your personal path in life. Your timing may be different from another's, but that doesn't make it any less perfect for you. So embrace the term perfection to mean the expression of your personal truth. Then you will no longer feel pressured to meet expectations that are inauthentic to you. Then you will be free to be yourself.

Know that you already are perfect by virtue of everything that makes up who you are. Perfection is subjective and open to interpretation. So don't strive for perfection. Just be yourself and you will find that your perfection is already within you. Strive not to meet some idealized standards that aren't even your own. Relax the pressure of trying to make yourself into something or someone you're not. Be compassionate with yourself and know that you are perfect in spite of your "mistakes" and perceived imperfections too. So if you mess up, learn from it, forgive yourself, and then move on knowing it's all part of your perfect journey.

Perfection is a state from which you came, and it is always who you are at your core. So make it your goal to simply be your best self, underneath all your masks and fronts and insecurities, and then you will find your personal brand of perfection that has been within you all along.

Alignment:

Also within the pages of this book you will come across the concept of alignment. Alignment here simply refers to the practice of being your most authentic self. It's a practice through which you choose to follow your truth, your purpose, and your inner confidence. It's a practice that allows you to use your free will to choose the thoughts, feelings, beliefs, and actions that are most aligned with your truth in every moment. So, to help you align with your true potential, each chapter of this book has been designed to give you a different perspective on how you can proactively align with who you truly are.

Furthermore, to help you better absorb the information you read in this book, and consequently align with your true self even faster, you will find various concepts emphasized. Note that this has been done with purpose; so that you can transform your negative beliefs that much faster into patterns of thought that work for you rather than against you. Know that the more you

You Are Here

absorb the information you read, and the more you apply it, the more benefit it will provide for you. And the more you understand it, the more aligned you will ultimately be.

Chapter 1:
What is Presence?

You are always in the here and now. Think about it, when are you ever anywhere else?

Presence is a state of being. It's a type of awareness that you have in the moment that causes you to be fully engaged in whatever you are thinking, feeling, and doing in that moment. It's a state through which you become truly empowered to create the life you want to live.

Presence is a realization that whatever you are initiating and whatever you are drawing forth into your life energetically and materially is always a result of your consciousness. So using your consciousness to dwell on the past or to worry about the future is simply counter-productive. Your point of power is always in the present moment. It's not in the past, because that's over with, and it's not in the future, because that's yet to come. You are always here and now. You are never truly anywhere else.

Being present means acknowledging your responsibilities, facing up to the issues in your life, and taking inspired action that's aligned with what you truly love. It's an inherent knowing that you have the power to positively affect your life experiences by being aware of what's going on within you and around you right now. As such, you can choose to make the present full of joy, faith, and trust.

Understand that you have choices in life. Things don't just happen to you, although on the surface it may appear as though they do. In truth, every moment gives you an opportunity to participate in what occurs in your life, and you are participating whether you are aware of it or not. As such, you are the one setting the tone for your own life experiences.

Your life experiences are simply a reflection of the dominant energy you're putting out into the world. As such, it makes sense to be conscious of your thought patterns, your feelings, and your subsequent actions so that you can be aware of what you are attracting into your life.

Being present allows you to fully experience each moment by bringing awareness to your thoughts, feelings, beliefs, and actions. You don't have to monitor your thoughts 24/7. Rather, simply use the present as your guide to help you understand what you are attracting into your life, and as such, to help you truly create the happiness you seek from the inside-out.

Don't let fear or uncertainty get the best of you because this will cause you to make hasty assumptions, as well as desperate attempts to predict the future and force or manipulate life's events into what you feel needs to happen. Know that we only try to control, force, and manipulate everything to go the way we think it "should" when we lack faith and trust in ourselves and in Divine Order.

The ego has a tough time with uncertainty because it means not always knowing what's ahead. As a result, being present in the face of uncertainty can sometimes feel uncomfortable and even intimidating. But you don't need to know every step ahead of time in order to trust that all is well. Just start with the step in front of you. Then one step at a time you will not only have arrived at your desired destination (or somewhere even better), but you will also have arrived through joyous means and in total faith.

Your life is a series of steps, each one playing a significant role in the bigger picture, each one leading you to the next one and the next. Realize that your life is not just about your final destination; it's about the experiences you have along the way. Every step and every moment is its own destination. Every moment is an opportunity to feel something, to create something, to enjoy something, and to share something. But it's up to you to choose the proactive route that's devoid of fear and full of love instead.

You have it in you to change your circumstances if you want to. All you need to do is change your consciousness right now and keep it focused in the right direction. Just use your feelings as your guide. Your feelings are of great value to you. We are often taught to stifle our feelings in fear of appearing vulnerable and weak. But what we frequently don't realize is that feelings are what actually empower us the most.

When you are aware of your feelings in the moment you are also aware of the thoughts that may be contradicting your truth and blocking your ultimate happiness. As such, you can use your feelings as feedback to help you adjust your thoughts and focus so that you are no longer thinking those unproductive thoughts that caused your negative feelings in the first place. Consequently, you will be able to take the reactive nature out of your behavior, and instead, make choices that are aligned with peace, love, and trust. When you understand what's going on within you, it's much easier to affect what's happening outside of you too.

As you start to use presence to your advantage you will recognize how empowered you truly are, and as a result, you will start to appreciate life a lot more. Being present is all about appreciation. It's about noticing what's around you, who's beside you, and the true self that's within you. It's about being aware of and appreciating the beauty that surrounds you; the beauty you often take for granted when you are in your rush to get things done.

Being present is also about being accepting of who you are and where you are in your life right now. It's about understanding that there are synchronicities occurring in your life in every moment, and as such, everything has its reason and purpose for you. Subsequently, presence is about being conscious enough to recognize the guidance you are being given in every moment from a part of you that knows best.

When you are present you are better able to relax into the flow of life because you can trust that you will always know what to do when the time is right. As such, you are more likely to be fully engaged in whatever you are doing in the moment, without worrying over how it will turn out. When you are present you do what you do for the sake of enjoying it and making the best of it in the moment, without being attached to a specific outcome or agenda.

You Are Here

Being present is about realizing the grandness of The Universe and the role you play in the bigger picture of life. It's about recognizing the scope of your purpose on this planet and the truth of who you are at your core. Being present is about being aware of your existence and the power you have in each moment to positively affect your life and the lives of others.

Being present is about understanding the truth of your inherent good. Know that what makes you good is not necessarily adhering to certain standards or principles. What makes you good is the simple fact that you are who you are right now. Meaning, what makes you good is the truth beneath all of your false identities, all of your hatred, all of your fears, all of your insecurities, all of your jealousies, and all of your ego-driven behaviors. What makes you inherently good is simply the fact that you are one with the Power of Creation, right now and always. But whether you express this truth or not is totally up to you.

We are all dynamic beings meant to experience total fulfillment. At our core, we are all deserving of love and the glorious, infinite bounty of The Universe. We are also all here to express something important. As such, being present is about infusing purpose into everything you do and with everyone you meet, simply because you know how powerful an impact this can have on the lives of others, not to mention your own. Being present is about joyously expressing your purpose and passions in ways that are authentic to you.

Being present is not about instant gratification. Rather, it's about recognizing the cause and effect relationship and how every decision you make has a profound effect on your life and the lives of those around you. It's about realizing that you have choices to make and that the choices you make right now will have an impact on what you experience not only in this moment, but in your future as well.

Now keep in mind, being present isn't about feeling pressured not to make a "mistake." Just because what you do now has an effect on your future doesn't mean you can't change your choices from moment to moment. Every moment is a new starting point so even if you feel you've taken a wrong turn

What is Presence?

somewhere, all you need to do is start over. Know that every moment is full of opportunity and possibility and that you can shift your momentum at any time simply by choosing to do so.

Being present is ultimately about trusting in the process of life and letting go of the need to control every detail. It's about knowing that you are cared and provided for, and it's about allowing yourself to be guided by an Infinite Wisdom that always has your best interest in mind. Simply learn to be more present in your moments and you will know what it means to truly live a blissful life.

APPLICATION:

The first thing you can do to practice the concept of presence in your life is to look at your life right now. Take this moment and truly think about where you are right now. Is it where you want to be? Is there something you'd like to change? Is there anything you can appreciate about your life right now?

Think about the current circumstances in your life and see them as feedback showing you where your consciousness has been thus far. Now keep in mind, if you're not quite where you want to be yet that doesn't necessarily mean you're blocking yourself from receiving what you desire. It may just be a matter of Divine Timing and going through a process. However, if you feel uneasy about an area of your life, or you instinctively feel that you are blocking yourself from achieving, or rather allowing what you want to manifest, then examine your beliefs about your deservingness and ability to have what you truly desire. Also, take a look at any patterns that have been reoccurring in your life and whether or not they have been serving you well or holding you back.

Check in with yourself to see if you are truly happy. If you're not, ask yourself, why not? What do you feel you need right now in order to be happy? Realize that you have everything you need to be happy right here and right now, and that it's simply a matter of perception.

Now take note of your feelings, understand them and proactively express them. Be aware of your inner climate of thoughts and feelings so that you can deal with how you truly feel, instead of repressing it. Understand that if you let your feelings bottle up they will likely cause you to react in a way you might later regret, or cause you to manifest something you'd rather not.

But when you are honest and aware of where you are and how you're feeling in the moment, you will then be in a better position to change your thoughts and actions accordingly to match the energy of where you actually want to be. By releasing resistance and shifting your focus onto those things that feel authentically good to you, you will not only end up feeling better, you will also ultimately shift the momentum of what you attract into your life.

What is Presence?

Presence is not only about being aware of where you are; it's also about being aware of what you love. So take note of your passions and your dreams. If you haven't had the courage to act on them yet, again, ask yourself, why not? What fears or regrets have been holding you back? Be honest. You can choose to live in ignorance and denial, but in doing so you will be choosing mediocrity and the same negative patterns that have led you to your lack of fulfillment thus far. Or, you can choose to be present and honest, which will get you onto your path of fulfillment a whole lot sooner. So which will you choose?

Presence is truly about appreciation. So if you're not happy, find something to appreciate. And if you are content and perhaps living your dreams right now, still find the time to appreciate every blessing in your life; not just your material gains and accomplishments, but the inner peace, joy, and true fulfillment you feel at your core. Realize the true source of your fulfillment (i.e. Source Energy) rather than taking it for granted. Ground yourself in your appreciation and share it rather than getting lost in the chase for more. By all means, continue to grow and expand, just remind yourself from time to time of how blessed you really are.

Furthermore, with all of your successes, notice the nature of each success and ask yourself if you are truly fulfilled from your soul, or if your fulfillment is being solely derived from your ego. Ask yourself what true fulfillment means to you and how you can start to express your true self right now, rather than giving in to the pressures others place on you, or the images and standards you feel you must live up to.

Be conscious of your choices. Don't allow your ego to lead you to impulsive decisions. Think before you act. You don't have to over-analyze everything. Just be aware of the energy you are putting out into the world. The next time you have an urge to react in a knee-jerk fashion, stop yourself and think of the potential consequences that behavior might have, think about where you might be over-reacting. Go ahead, feel what you feel, just know in the moment how powerful your thoughts and feelings really are. Don't let your ego drive you to react in a way that you'll later regret. Understand the power of the present moment and instead of falling into old negative patterns that no longer serve you, use that power wisely to create the life you truly want to live.

Chapter 2:
Taking a Time-Out

Increasing your speed won't necessarily get you "there" any faster.

Do you ever feel like you're on the gerbil wheel of life, running in circles but getting nowhere fast?

Sure, life can sometimes feel like a juggling act. It can certainly feel stressful looking at your daily to-do list, knowing that there are only 24 hours in a day and wondering how you can possibly get it all done. It's no wonder we're so fixated on the past and the future; the present can sometimes feel quite overwhelming. Wondering about what might have been or fantasizing about what's to come are great ways to avoid the present, but eventually we have to deal with "what is." And in fact, it is through accepting and dealing with "what is" that allows for what's best to manifest.

Life is not meant to be a struggle. Life is not just one big check-list. There has to be more meaning to it than that. Sure, life is about getting things done, but it's certainly not the only thing that's important. You will never really get everything done anyway because there will always be more to do, but that's the fun thing about life; it's not just about getting somewhere or doing something, it's about enjoying the path that you're on and breathing in the moments along the way.

While it's certainly good practice to take a time-out from the hectic pace of life on a general basis, it's that much more important to do so when you're feeling overwhelmed and stressed-out. In fact, if you're burnt-out, not only will nothing get done, it will only add to your frustration. It's simple; you cannot function at your most efficient pace if you are exhausted and rundown.

Taking a time-out, then, is simply about taking the time to breathe. It's about being aware of the holistic system that makes up who you truly are. You are body, you are mind, and you are spirit, and all of these facets are vitally important to your overall well-being.

So take good care of yourself. This means nourishing your body with healthy foods, making time for exercise, engaging in positive communications and cultivating loving relationships, nurturing your passions, sharing (giving and receiving), and taking the time to relax, contemplate, meditate, clear your mind, and even reflect on who you are and what you truly want out of life. As you devote time to each of these aspects of your being you will notice yourself feeling more energized, more at peace, and happier than ever before. You'll also find yourself getting a lot more done more effectively and efficiently than you had in the past.

Know that our bodies are designed to express total harmony and well-being, our minds are designed to make free choices, and our spirits are designed to be infinite. At our core we are designed to receive everything we need in life without having to struggle for it or fight to get it. It is when we work with our holistic system and find harmony from within that we are able to function at our maximum capacity and allow our fulfillment to surface with ease and joy. As such, taking a time-out helps us restore our harmony, which also gets us back into the flow of life.

Keep in mind, a time-out doesn't necessarily mean going off to some remote mountain top for months at a time. A time-out can simply mean taking a walk at lunch, enjoying a cup of tea, playing with your dog, having a nice dinner with a loved-one, reading a good book, or whatever it is that you enjoy doing. The key, however, is to be fully present while doing it. If you are thinking about a million other things at the same time, you are missing the point of this exercise.

You may think that with all your responsibilities you cannot afford to take a time-out. But in truth, you cannot afford not to. Taking a time-out actually makes you more productive in the long run. When you approach things with a new perspective and a refreshed outlook, the quality of what you do sky-rockets. But if you keep pushing yourself beyond exhaustion, the quality of what you do will eventually suffer. So you would be doing yourself, your work, and others a great service by choosing to take the time to care for yourself.

It's important to keep in mind that the point of taking a time-out isn't to escape your responsibilities. Rather, it is to regroup and refresh yourself so that you can make smarter choices. It's about finding balance and harmony in your life and taking the time to nurture every aspect of yourself. It's about respecting and loving yourself so that you can genuinely respect and love others as well. You can only give what you have, but if you feel lacking, you'll simply feel like you have nothing to give. So make sure you are full of joy and love in each moment and you will have that much more to share with the world.

APPLICATION:

Write down at least 10 things that you love to do. For instance, you could list your hobbies, your dreams, your passions, and basically anything you love to do or want to do. You can also keep adding to your list. Don't limit yourself. It can be something you feel is relatively common, like enjoying your morning cup of tea, or something perceivably more involved, like owning your own business, traveling the world, being a successful author/singer/actor/scientist, or whatever the case may be.

Now create a schedule for yourself where you make time for doing at least one of these things at least once a day. You can do a lot of it, you can do a little of it. You can spend time visualizing it, getting it started, keeping it going, or whatever steps you feel like taking in the moment. Whatever it is that you love, do something with it each and every day, but make sure you are being authentic with it and doing it out of love and joy rather than obligation or agenda.

Be mindful of the present moment as you are doing these things. Don't allow yourself to be distracted by notions of anything other than what you are doing right in that moment. Put your all into it. Enjoy it. Savor it without thinking about what the outcome will be. Just enjoy the moment and take in the experience for its own sake. Make sure you are not fixated on any other outcome or result. Release your expectations, attachments, and agendas. The results will come, but in the meantime, you can simply enjoy the experience of the moment.

Too often we get fixated on an end result. We plow our way through to get there, but in doing so we miss out on the joy of the experience, on the lessons, and on other opportunities. And often when we get to where we thought we wanted to be, we still fail to be satisfied. But a time-out is not about an end result. A time-out is not meant to create pressure or stress. A time-out is meant to bring joy and expression back into your life. So let your focus be on enjoying your experience in the present moment, and let the rest unfold naturally.

Taking a Time-Out

Taking a time-out needn't be complicated. A simple way of taking a time-out is to literally breathe. Breathing is something we do constantly but often take for granted. By taking a moment to notice your breath you instantly place yourself in a time-out. Consequently, doing this can be an excellent way of de-stressing and grounding yourself in the present moment. It can also help you gather your composure and clear your mind.

All you need to do is be aware of your in-breath and your out-breath, without trying to force it. Just notice it; notice the air as it moves in and out of your body. In that moment let your entire focus revolve around your breath and nothing else. Thoughts may come and go, but keep your focus on that very moment, feeling the Life Force moving through every part of you.

You can also take a time-out by engaging your senses. Sit for a moment and actively bring your attention to the sounds you hear, the aromas in the air, the colors all around you, the textures you feel, the tastes you experience, etc. Be fully aware of where you are, how you are feeling, and what you are experiencing right in that moment. Then just be with it, without judgments, without labels. Just be. Engage all your senses and make a conscious effort to focus on what you are experiencing with each one. This will help you develop your awareness, and the more you practice this awareness, the more positive power you will ultimately cultivate.

Taking a time-out is about finding fulfillment in the little things as well as the bigger things, in the details, and in the journey. So take a time-out and notice how this joy carries over into all other areas of your life as well. Notice how you have more patience and more enthusiasm. Notice how your energy shifts when you take time to value and honor your soul's desires. Notice how much happier you are and how that also benefits those around you. Know that it is never selfish to genuinely love and care about yourself, for it is in this care that you fill yourself up with the energy you ultimately share with others.

Don't ever feel guilty for taking a time-out for yourself. Know that it benefits all those in your life just as much as it benefits you. It is when you are happy that you have happiness to share. So go ahead and feed your soul, for you are here to accomplish great things and to enjoy your life, fulfill your purpose, and share your truth and love with the world.

Chapter 3:
One with Nature

Look to nature and you will see your own perfection being mirrored back at you.

One of the best ways to get present fast is to get grounded in nature. When you realize that you too are of nature, you will feel connected to everything you see. When you pay attention to the perfect order within nature, you will realize that you too are part of that perfection. Nothing happens in vain; everything serves its purpose.

Observing nature is very sobering. The only thing that nature is ever concerned with is the present moment. It is not worried about what it will eat tomorrow, how it will grow, what the rain and wind will do to its existence. It just is, right now. If you observe nature you will notice how the Life Force flows generously through it, guiding it gently to what it needs to do and where it needs to be. But nature does not resist. Instead it goes with the flow with total surrender and trust.

Nature is powered by the same Life Force that governs everything else that exists. As such, this Life Force moves through each and every one of us too. So, just as nature does, we can learn to let go and allow ourselves to flow with ease and without worry.

Just because we have the consciousness and free will to make our own choices in life doesn't mean we need to abuse or misuse this gift, and in turn, cause our own suffering. Yes, we have the ability to make free choices (in our perceptions, with our actions, through our focus, etc.), but within these choices we also have the option of allowing ourselves to flow like nature does, in perfect time and order. We can choose to fight against nature and allow our false selves to create chaos in our lives, or we can choose to flow with the Life Force that moves nature and live a life full of trust, guidance, and total fulfillment.

The streams do not worry about the rocks in their way; they naturally move around them, sometimes through them, to create new, stronger paths. Tree branches do not stand firm fighting against the wind; they bend with the breeze with flexibility. We too have this ability. We need to look to nature for inspiration, for within nature there are a great deal of lessons to learn and miracles and wonders to admire.

Nature does not stand in its own way. The grass grows with ease, the flowers bloom like clockwork, and the birds know when to fly south for the winter. Nature knows, and so do we. But nature is only ever doing what it does in the present moment. It only concerns itself with today and right now. It trusts its order and does not worry about what's to come.

This is a lesson we can apply into our own lives. We too can learn how to let go and let nature take its course. We do not need to be passive. We simply need to know when we are standing in our own way, and then clear our path to fulfillment. We too can allow ourselves to be guided by the very force that is guiding nature so well. It's a matter of recognizing the peace and order within nature and allowing ourselves to consciously become one with it.

Observe nature and you will soon realize that there is a Grand Powerful Energy that moves it on all levels. It is inspiring, influencing, guiding, and nudging nature to do its thing. Nature doesn't protest, but it all seems to work out just fine nonetheless. Take your cue from nature and you will know what it means to live with presence, peace, and flow.

APPLICATION:

Devote some time for taking a walk in a park or sitting within nature and just being one with it. You can even simply look out through your window and observe nature at work. Observe what's around you. Listen to the birds singing, notice the wind as it rustles through the leaves, observe the bees pollinating the flowers, and so on. Feel the freedom, feel the oneness, feel the order, feel the perfection of what you are experiencing right in the moment.

By being present in this way you will become aware of the bigger picture. You will notice how you are a part of it too. You will realize how effortless your journey can be if you just let go of your need to control everything and everyone. Observe how nature is not trying to manipulate anything. Know that you don't need to either.

Do this every day. Use it as a grounding exercise for when you feel disconnected, or just to remind yourself of who and what you are at your core. Allow yourself to embrace the flow that is running through everything so beautifully. Notice how everything has a purpose and know that you are no different.

This can also be a good time to pose any questions for which you would like guidance. And it's a good time to listen to what your higher-self has to tell you.

Spending just a few minutes a day observing nature is enough to ground and relax you so that you can make your best decisions. Feeling your oneness with nature brings everything into perspective, and as such, it leads you to experience a more relaxed, joyous, and peaceful existence.

Chapter 4:

Slowing Down

Life is not a race. Slow down so that your dreams can catch up with you.

So what does slowing down really mean? Well, it's not about being lazy and it's not about underachieving. It's not even about lacking ambition. Rather, it's more about getting into your personal rhythm and not allowing outside pressures to influence your choices. It's about doing what you do in each moment at a pace that's right for you. It's about understanding that rushing towards results causes more stress than it does peace.

It's simple really. When you are in a rush and living outside of the present moment you are more prone to anxiety and more likely to make impulsive decisions, which may end up costing you more time and effort in the long run. Slowing down does not mean you stop taking action; slowing down simply means going with the natural flow of life and not trying to rush the process. It's a different type of action. It's action that comes out of confidence, patience, and certainty rather than fear, doubt, and insecurity.

Slowing down is also about trust. It's about being accepting of the present moment and releasing your attachments to the outcome of things. It's about doing what you do with pleasure rather than out of obligation. It's about knowing your priorities and choosing what's absolutely necessary to do in the moment, resolving to take care of everything else as it comes.

Slowing down is about knowing when to do something yourself and when to share responsibility or delegate to others. One of the reasons why we are so stressed-out these days is because we choose to take upon ourselves way more than we need to. Sometimes we think we're the only ones who can do what needs to get done, but often this comes from our own need to control rather than from any actual truth. In fact, there are many equally viable ways to get things done.

Subsequently, slowing down long enough to realize that you need help frees up your time to do more of what you love to do. Understand that you don't need to be an expert at everything. There are people out there who would gladly do what you don't absolutely love, so let them. This way each person has the chance to express their talents and skills and everyone ends up happy and fulfilled. Sure, sometimes you'll need to learn a new skill and/or take on a new project; just know when you're doing it out of joy, and when you're taking it on because you're too afraid to give up control.

When you take the time to truly understand and acknowledge what brings you the most joy, you become better able to enjoy yourself in every moment. You begin to savor and appreciate everything you do because you are now doing it out of joy rather than dread. Slowing down, then, is really about appreciating the moment before you, and choosing your actions based on your authenticity rather than your ego.

Slowing down enables you to appreciate the food you eat, the summer breeze on your face, the smell of a flower's fresh scent, or whatever else you are experiencing in the moment. In this state of appreciation you are also able to trust that all will get done in good time, and in turn, you are able to focus on the quality and value of what you are giving, receiving, and doing in each moment.

Look at each task in your life as an opportunity to do something great. This change in perspective will then positively affect the outcome of everything you do. Perceive everything as a choice, rather than as a chore or obligation, and you will appreciate and even enjoy all that you do that much more.

Give yourself the gift of time. Chances are you have more of it than you think. Really examine what's truly necessary and prioritize well. If you do, you will likely find places where you spend more time worrying and stressing, complaining and whining, comparing and competing, than you do actually accomplishing anything productive. Most likely you will also find responsibilities you have unnecessarily taken upon yourself that you could easily delegate to others.

Slowing down means being mindful of what you want in life and finding the smartest ways of taking action on it, in whatever ways feel right to you in the moment. When you slow down your hectic pace you allow peace and productivity to emerge. When you slow down you find smart solutions and you make smart choices.

Everyone has their own stride. The important thing is not to compare yourself to others or try to meet someone else's expectations based on what they think you "should be" doing or how quickly you "should be" doing it. Find the pace that works best for you and find a method that allows you to meet your timelines without stressing yourself out.

Slowing down is about releasing pressure and expectations and just following your authentic bliss in each moment. At the end of the day you'll find that when you are having fun, or at the very least, making the most of every situation, you will likely end up getting things done much more efficiently and much more enjoyably than if you act out of tension and stress.

Understand that your personal stride is devoid of stress. Actually, you can determine whether or not you've found your stride by assessing the level of stress you feel on a day to day basis. Your authentic pace is not something that is based in ego. It is not something that causes you stress. Rather, it is something that invigorates you, excites you, and nourishes you. Slowing down in this instance means moving at the pace that best suits you rather than trying to match someone else's pace that's inauthentic to you. It means finding your personal stride where you can enjoy what you're doing rather than feeling overwhelmed by it.

With that said, it's important to note that slowing down in this context is less about speed and more about awareness. Maybe you're a person who works well under pressure, someone who thrives within a fast-paced environment? If this is your authentic pace, something you feel good about, and it's something that resonates with your soul (rather than being motivated by fear, doubt, impatience, or other ego emotions), then go for it. It's a matter of being honest with yourself and choosing a pace that feels right to you rather than pretending to be someone you're not.

Slowing down doesn't necessarily mean slowing your actual pace. While it can mean this, often it means simply cutting out unnecessary worry by reassessing your priorities and adopting a proactive and positive attitude. It can mean taking a breather if you feel stressed-out or at a loss for what to do. It can mean slowing down your mind long enough to make the most proactive choices rather than being influenced by external pressures.

Slowing down is really about being authentic and operating at your most effective pace, manner, and stride. Only you know when you've reached that pace, and when you do, you will have found your unique path in life. Practice different methods until you find the one that feels right to you. Pay no attention to others' negative opinions of your method, or whether or not they approve of it. Be open to feedback and be willing to make adjustments, but also trust in your own method and trust in yourself. If it's working for you, and it's helping you make a better contribution, that's all that matters. Be an example to others of what it's like to follow your own path and have it work for you.

You do not need to succumb to the pressures others place on you, or spend your time seeking their approval. The more time you waste worrying over hypothetical situations and responses, or being angry or anxious, the less you will be allowing your solutions to come forth. So release your worries and allow yourself to relax into the flow of life. Let solutions come into your awareness so that you can make proactive choices and take inspired actions.

Slowing down is really about taking conscious action when your energy moves you to do so. Forcing yourself to do something you perceive as a chore will only deprive the task of your full commitment, not to mention the full benefit that can come of it. Acting when your energy moves you isn't a license to procrastinate. It's simply about releasing any resistance you may have

Slowing Down

towards the fulfillment you desire by injecting joy into whatever it is that you do. You want your actions to be inspired. Acting when your energy moves you is one way to ensure that you are taking action out of love and joy and choice rather than resentment, obligation, or fear.

When you slow your hectic pace for just a moment you start to recognize any resistance you may be creating within you in that moment. As such, you become empowered to change your thoughts, feelings, beliefs, and actions so that they match the truth of who you are rather than your fears and insecurities about who you're not.

Understand that anything that causes resistance within you blocks the fulfillment you seek to experience. Awareness, however, can solve all that. It gets you present-focused, and as such, it deflates your resistance by bringing consciousness into the mix. This consciousness then allows you to not only be aware of what's going on within you, but also to understand and transform the thoughts, feelings, and beliefs that are causing your resistance in the first place.

Relax the pressure and act when your spirit, not your ego, moves you. But know that not all pressure is bad. Sometimes we need something to nudge us out of our ego's comfort zone. Sometimes the pressure we receive is in fact The Universe guiding us in the right direction. Your job is to figure out which pressure motivates you and which stresses you out.

Do what ultimately feels good to your soul. Your life is meant to be joyous, not torturous, so find a way to play. Find a way to bring back the joy in all that you do. Be honest with yourself and stop allowing your ego to rule your pace in life. Find your soul's pace instead and you will be assured of peace, success, and happiness in all areas of life.

APPLICATION:

Slowing down is about finding your personal stride and flow. So ask yourself, "What pace truly feels good to me?" If you take away all the pressures and expectations that others place on you, and even those you place on yourself, what are you left with?

In order to figure out your personal pace it's important that you prioritize well. The more you understand your priorities, the easier it will be for you to step into your personal flow and distinguish between what you really need to do, and what tasks are simply taking up your time unnecessarily.

So make a daily list of what you feel you need to get done. Now rank this list in order of importance or immediacy. Once you have done this, pinpoint the things on that list that you can bring yourself to delegate. Even if there's nothing you can delegate, at the very least you will know what is highest in priority rather than wasting time trying to juggle it all at once.

Often we feel overwhelmed because we try to do too many things at once, or perhaps fit ourselves into others' schedules too much. So if you feel that the pace that's expected of you is beyond the pace you feel comfortable with, know that there is always a solution that will work for all involved. You just have to be honest from the start, and stay honest, even if/when conditions change.

Sometimes in our attempt to please others and meet deadlines we multi-task too much. While some people are good multi-taskers, some just aren't. So by prioritizing and then placing your attention on one thing at a time you will find your own pace, and be able to work within another's pace as well.

No one's pace is better or worse, just different. So figure out even within another's pace what pace works best for you. Focus on the task at hand and don't let your fears or worries distract you. Know that there is always a way to get things done in a way that feels good to you, even when complying with another's timeline. Simply communicate what you need while also listening to the needs of others. Know that worrying and pressuring yourself will only cause you to waste energy that could be used to accomplish what you need to do. Start by slowing your worries and you will find the way that works best for all concerned.

Understand that the time you spend stressing and worrying is the time you take away from living your joy in each and every moment. You need to decide what's most important to you and give yourself permission to just be with it. Release your worries and strict expectations of yourself. This will free up more of your time, because your worries, doubts, and fears can create a lot of wasted time and scattered energy. If you are not focused on worry, doubt, or fear then you will have more energy to devote to doing what you love.

Also, ask yourself how much of what you do is just to please others? How much of it is authentic to what you want, and how much of it is being done for the sake of getting approval? Knowing this will help you recognize what you really want to express and do, and it will also help you make time for it because you will realize that it's a priority for you.

Slowing down is about making time for what's important to you. It's about recognizing what you want out of life and then taking inspired action towards it. But don't make commitments you are not willing to keep because that will only waste your time and the time of others. Don't waste your time backtracking and making excuses. Instead, decide on your priorities and then back your words with actions. This way you will not be wasting your moments away with faulty promises, guilt, or regret.

Be honest about what you need from others, but be respectful of what others need as well. If you feel pressured to meet another's expectations of you, let it be known. Don't hold it inside and push yourself to do something you know you're not ready to commit to. Recognize what you are willing to do and be proactive about voicing that. This way you won't be wasting your moments with trying to explain yourself, and you won't be disappointing anyone as a result. Slowing down is about being honest with yourself and with others so that every moment you spend is spent doing what you authentically love without it being at the expense of another.

Slowing down is about recognizing when a change is needed in your life, but it's also about having the courage to make that change. It's about acknowledging your weak areas and then doing something about them. But if you are rushing around and running away you will never truly know where change is needed. Know that you can never run away from yourself anyway. You can change your surroundings and you can change up the people in your life, but you can never escape yourself. So instead, slow down and face yourself, face your fears, face your insecurities, face your doubts, and then make the commitment to transform yourself into the best self you can be.

Furthermore, slowing down is about living a life of harmony and fulfillment. In order to do so, however, you must give attention to all areas of your life. So recognize right now what each area of your life needs in order to be whole. What or whom have you been neglecting? Recognize where your attention is needed, and then make the commitment to follow-through on that. Respect and honor every aspect and area of your life because each one deserves your attention.

Slowing down is also about being open to asking for and receiving help rather than turning yourself into a martyr. While you are unlimited in what you can do, there is no shame in asking for help. Any pressure or stress you feel is most likely caused by you trying to do more than you need to all by yourself, running at a pace that's inauthentic to you, being unwilling to ask for help out of pride or a need to control, and/or having a need for others' approval. But you can choose to let go of all that.

Slowing down doesn't mean being lazy or complacent. It simply means having trust and faith, releasing your need to control, and most importantly, enjoying yourself with whatever you are doing. It means being smart with your time and not wasting it away with worry, doubt, or fear.

When we are stressed our thoughts begin to race. So if this happens to you, just slow yourself down. Slow your thoughts and direct your focus onto something that feels authentically good to you in the moment. Change things up a bit. Take your attention away from what's worrying you. As a result, this will help you change your momentum from stress to bliss.

You can also choose to simply focus on others. Ask someone what you can do for them today. Go out of your way to be sharing with others, without any agendas, attachments, or expectations. This will slow down your worries and allow you to not only help others, but also to change your own perspective, thereby allowing the solutions you seek to freely flow to you.

Slowing down allows you to be aware of your own reactive behaviors as well as it gives you time to contemplate your actions and the potential effects those actions will have. Slowing down allows you to make proactive choices that work best for you as well as for others. So whenever you feel stressed, just stop, breathe, and assess what's really going on. This does not necessarily mean stop doing. It does not mean be lazy. It simply means be aware of and appreciate what you are doing in the present moment and how you feel about it.

Do your best to make the most of each moment. Understand that stress comes from your perceptions and choices in life. No matter what you have going on around you know that you always have a choice. Slowing down is about making proactive choices, deciding on what you're ready to commit to doing, and then following through on that. But it's also about recognizing when you don't really want to do something, and then figuring out the best course of action to take with regards to that task. So, if you're facing a task that you don't feel like doing in the moment, here are some options you can consider:

1. Let it go and resolve to do it later when you feel inspired to do so and when you can fully commit to it. This is better than doing it with resentment or dread.
2. Change your perspective about it so that you can freely do it now and feel good about it.
3. Find another way of doing it that feels authentically better to you, or simply do something else that makes more sense to you.
4. Ask for help or delegate it.

It's important, however, that you understand why you don't feel like doing something in the moment, and that you check in with yourself to make sure it's not your ego influencing you. So keep this in mind when choosing from the options above, and make sure that you are being motivated by your true self first and foremost.

It's also important to note here that sometimes others will be depending on your follow-through, so be conscious of when you are making commitments, and most importantly, only make commitments that you are willing and able to fulfill. Then be sure to do so with the right perspectives and intentions in mind. So instead of feeling pressured to so something, feel privileged to have the opportunity of doing it. Be happy that you are providing someone with what they need. Be proud of being trust-worthy and reliable. The reward you get from follow-through is really its own treasure.

When you slow down to reach your personal pace in life you will realize that your life is about choice, and you will naturally feel less stressed and freer to do what you love. Once you slow the pressures you place on yourself you will realize that your life really can be about peace and joy. All you need is to make that conscious decision to do what you love, while also learning to compromise and share with others. All you need is to decide to be the best you that you can be. In truth, it is when everyone is honest and authentic to their own stride that we all end up satisfied.

Chapter 5:
Being Present in the Face of Technology

True human contact can never be replaced. While we can compress our schedules and computerize our interactions, life as a whole cannot be digitized; it's far too advanced for that.

This topic is of particular importance, especially in today's world. Over the last century we have advanced a great deal technologically speaking but it's not quite evident if we are handling this technology in the best way.

The aim of technology is to make our lives easier, simpler, and more efficient. Its intention is to allow us to communicate faster, better, and smoother with each other. Its purpose is to bring us together rather than distance us. Unfortunately, sometimes the way we use our technology does indeed create walls between us.

Our technological conveniences can cause a disconnection between us if we don't use them proactively. Understand that this disconnect occurs not necessarily when we use technology, but rather when we let our technology use us.

Being present in the face of technology simply means knowing why you are using it, being conscious as you are using it, and being aware of when it's using you. It means benefiting from the advantages of it without losing sight of what's most important in the moment. You must be in control of your technology; it cannot be the other way around. You need to discipline yourself so that using technology doesn't become a means of escaping your life or feeding into one instant gratification after another.

It's important to clarify that the context we are discussing here has more to do with the abuse of technology than the proactive use of it. It is particularly relevant to those who have allowed their lives to be taken over by it, those who feel isolated because of it, and those who are feeling stressed as a result of the increased demands it has put on their lives.

Of course technology is a great convenience that provides many means and methods for connection and enjoyment. The point here, however, is to simply point out that we need to be responsible with it so that we do not sacrifice our authentic human interactions as a result of it, and so that we do not create more stress and pressure in our lives due to it.

When we are not disciplined with our technology we tend to get consumed by it. New pressures arise to be faster in all that we do. We become expected to be available and on-call 24/7 for the most trivial of things. We then use our technology to escape rather than engage, and to feed into our growing boredom and disdain for what's actually in front of us. It becomes a means of feeding an ego fix rather than helping us genuinely connect with one another. As a result, we end up taking for granted that which is most important. Our focus then goes on everywhere else but the present moment.

There's a time and place for using technological mediums, and sometimes right here and now is most appropriate, but we mustn't lose perspective on what's truly important. Ask yourself if your next email or text message is something that matters right now, or if it is your need for instant gratification that's propelling you to act. Is it the most optimal way of connecting at this time, or is there a better way? Are you trying to avoid something in the moment by distracting yourself with nonsensical or trivial "conversations," or are you truly engaged in what you are doing? Are you hiding behind emails and texts because you're too afraid to face someone? What's going on in this moment right now that truly needs your undivided attention and total commitment?

It's not that technology is negative. On the contrary, it makes our lives better in many ways. It's just that there needs to be an effort made to learn how to use it properly without losing the human connection, and without losing our presence, awareness, and appreciation for where we are right now. If we allow impatience, and the resulting instant gratification, to run our lives, we will be on the continual search for fix after fix, and we will be more likely to make impulsive decisions that will inevitably lead us to undesirable consequences.

Advancement is necessary and it's a natural part of life, but as our technology evolves, our consciousness must evolve with it. It's not about regression. It's about realization. It's about making sure that we are in control of our behavior. The point is, if you are feeling stressed and pulled in a million directions, it may be time to re-assess how much power your technology actually has over you. Are you the one leading the way, or do your gadgets have a mind of their own?

When you are in control of your technology you know when to use it and when to put it away. But if you are over-consumed with it you may end up missing out on the beauty of your present moments. There is a time and place; figure out which is which for you.

Being present in the face of technology is about being aware of your surroundings and your feelings in the moment. It's about appreciating what you have right in front of you. It's about allowing yourself to rest from all the distractions that are supposedly there to simplify your life. This is not an advocacy to give up technology. This is not a campaign to eliminate the conveniences of life. It is simply an urging for you to wake up to what's going on around you; to be conscious about life and considerate of other people. It's a recommendation for those who complain about being stressed and over-worked to look at the amount of time they spend with their gadgets over the quality of time they spend with their true selves, their surroundings, and the people in their lives.

Being present in the face of technology is ultimately about prioritizing your life. It's about creating a system that allows you to consciously use the technology at hand without losing your joy and appreciation for what's going on around you and within you. You need to discipline yourself and learn to be in control of your habits rather than having them control you. You need to figure out a way that marries your technological conveniences with appreciating, respecting, and enjoying the value within each present moment.

So get present and consider the amount of attention you are truly giving to what is right in front of you, and to those with whom you are spending time. Ask yourself, "Are my actions and interactions sincere or are they robotic?" "Am I using my technology proactively or am I addicted to it?" Answer honestly and your answers will open up the door to more revelations about what you may be hiding from or avoiding, and what's truly blocking you from the life you want to live.

So if you want to improve the quality of your life and increase your overall happiness, simply bring yourself back into the present moment. Bring yourself back to appreciating your true freedom. Use your technology wisely and it will work for you rather than against you. Bottom line, know when to use it and know when to shut it down.

APPLICATION:

For about a week or so, be aware of how much time you spend using social media, emailing, texting, etc. A good way to keep track of this is to start a journal and jot down on average how much time you spend on these various activities. Also, notice how much of what you are doing is authentic and how much of it is a matter of impatience, avoidance, or a need to fill time with instant gratification. For this week all you need to do is notice and be aware. You do not have to change your habits yet, just become conscious of them.

Once you've realized your habits, the next step is to understand whether they contribute to or take away from your true satisfaction in life. What's truly motivating your actions? Do your habits cause you stress? Do they take away from the quality of your relationships and interactions? Are they helping you avoid something you actually need to face? Take a look at each one of your habits and rate them by level of true satisfaction that they bring to your life. What are the pros and what are the cons? Do they add to your true fulfillment or are they causing you more stress than benefit?

When you've come to understand which habits are benefiting you versus those that are a detriment to you, your next step will be to cut down on those habits that are causing you stress by making a willing choice to joyfully reduce your participation in them.

At the end of the day, the choices you make are what impact your life and the lives of those around you. Choosing to add more quality to your life benefits everyone. The key is to set priorities and healthy boundaries so that you are no longer at the mercy of your bad habits, and so that you are no longer being insincere with your actions. Do not do things out of obligation or as a means to escape your reality. Choose to be present and make the most of each moment for this is what will ultimately add to the quality of your life.

Sit with yourself for a few moments enjoying your own presence. Be engaged in the time you spend with friends and family. Savor the moment at hand and be conscious of your choices and the motivations behind them.

Do not feed into your need for instant gratification. Do not feed into others' impatience and need for instant gratification either. It's up to you to set your own boundaries and then uphold them. If anything, others will value and respect you more for standing your ground and respecting yourself. They may even follow your lead.

Often times we feel the need to be immediately responsive out of fear that we will miss out on an opportunity, but it's often our fear itself that causes this to be so. We have grown so accustomed to demanding what we want when we want it that our capacity for patience has begun to suffer. But patience is amazing. Through it we can realize what we really want in life, and how to make it so.

Through patience we give ourselves the opportunity to make proactive choices out of thoughtfulness rather than recklessness. So when you refuse to be a prisoner of your technology by being aware of and present with what you are thinking, feeling, and doing, you give yourself the time to consider the options that work best. And because you are patient, what is best is free to come into your awareness.

So if you feel fear creeping up on you, practice patience, trust, and appreciation instead. Trust that the opportunities that are right for you will be there for you in one way or another. We are all blessed with amazing conveniences these days, but in order to show our appreciation and continue to evolve in the right direction we must learn the true value of what we have available to us, and how to use it best.

Understand that taking some time to stop and appreciate your present moments will not take you away from what is truly yours and coming to you. Sure, sometimes immediate action may be required, in which case you'll have to respond to the demand of the moment. But action taken out of trust and faith rather than fear and doubt is far more proactive and productive. So trust that any opportunity that is truly good for you, worth your while, and aligned with your purpose will never compromise your integrity, your authenticity, or your self-respect.

Being Present in the Face of Technology

Take a moment right now and think about what actions you've been taking lately that are based in fear, obligation, and/or impatience. Be honest with yourself because the more honest you are, the faster you will be able to clear your bad habits and create the life you want to live.

Take a look at how you use your technology and how sincere your communications really are. For instance, emails, text messages, social media, and the like have become an all too convenient way of hiding from real human contact and true interest in what others are feeling. They have become a superficial way of "staying in touch" without really being in touch at all. And if we let them, these mediums will collectively feed into our short attention spans and false need for instant gratification, which will only contribute to the disconnection between us.

There is undoubtedly a time and place for these modes of communication, and they can certainly be a great means for staying informed and connected with people from all over the world. However, if you truly want to experience quality in your life you need to determine when convenience is more important, and when it's more pertinent to take it to the next level and form deeper connections. Be honest about your communications and recognize when they are superficial and when they are really founded in something more substantial.

Make it a priority in your life to create quality interactions. When you spend time with people, really notice and appreciate them. If you make plans to see a friend or have dinner with family, turn that into quality time. Refrain from engaging in activities that distract you from the experience and joy of that present moment. Engage in conversations and truly be there and present. Make sure not to lose the human connection, which is truly the reason for much of our technology in the first place, i.e. to make it easier for us to connect.

Know that technology is replaceable but that people are not. Know that each moment in your life deserves your full attention. So if you don't truly need it in the moment, put it away. Commit to really being present in all of your interactions and all of your activities, and true fulfillment will find its way to you.

Chapter 6:
Contemplation and Awareness

Making positive choices comes naturally when your awareness is grounded in truth.

Our society today is largely motivated by reactivity. We react to the news, we react to other people, and we react to essentially everything that happens to us. Unfortunately, all this reaction causes us to become part of the problem rather than the solution. We react to all of the circumstances in our lives but we fail to take the time to understand the role we play in what we manifest. As a result, we end up living from one happenstance to another, waiting for the other shoe to drop, and feeling like victims in the process. But we can put an end to all of this.

By being present, and subsequently aware and contemplative, we have the opportunity to awaken ourselves to the potential effects our actions will have on our lives, and as such, empower ourselves to participate in the creation process of what we experience here on this earth. In a nutshell, being present, aware, and contemplative simply means the difference between living a robotic, reactive existence, and living a conscious and creative life.

There is a difference, however, between contemplation and over-analysis. Over-analysis is self-indulgent. It stems from fear, doubt, and insecurity. It propels you to obsessively worry over the meaning of everything, which can consequently lead to procrastination and stagnation.

Contemplation, on the other hand, is about making proactive assessments in the moment that are devoid of worry and doubt. It's about considering the effects of your actions and making informed and intuitive choices rather than robotic ones. Contemplation is about understanding your internal climate and then proactively choosing focus and actions that are aligned with your authentic self.

Contemplation is not about indulging your ego, thinking only of "What's in it for me?" Contemplation is about understanding your contribution to the world. It's about understanding the impact your thoughts, words, feelings, and actions will have on other people, as well as yourself. Contemplation is about considering the potential effects your actions will have before they occur.

Awareness and contemplation go hand-in-hand. In order to contemplate anything you need to first be aware of it. Then once you are aware, you automatically become grounded in the present moment. And when you are grounded in this way you then enable yourself to make smart choices that are attuned to your higher-self and higher purpose.

Through awareness, and subsequent follow-through, you empower yourself to create the life you want to live. It is when you dwell on the past, obsess about the future, or engage in numerous distractions within your present moments that you rob yourself of the experience of the now, and all the potential for true joy and fulfillment that lies therein.

While awareness plays a vital role in your path to self-empowerment, it may feel like a daunting task to keep up. By nature our minds wander and our attention wavers. But this is exactly why we need to get into the practice of bringing ourselves into the present moment, for it is in the present moment that we gain clarity, focus, and order.

Self-empowerment starts with choice. So start by choosing to be positive and optimistic in all of your perceptions. Continue choosing positive focus, making sure it's genuinely aligned with the truth of who you really are at your core. Then, as you stay focused on what's true, you will be creating for yourself a life full of peace and joy.

Know that wherever your attention goes, your manifesting power goes with it. So the more aware you are of your focus and how you're feeling in the moment, the more purposeful your manifesting power becomes. You can then choose to direct and align your thoughts so that they magnetize to you that which you truly love from a place of inner joy, trust, and authentic expression.

Contemplation and Awareness

When you are aware of your inner drive, i.e. the motives behind all that you do, you become more empowered with all that you manifest. Contemplation and awareness, then, are simply about understanding your motives and choosing to act out of inspiration rather than fear. It's about knowing that if the energy behind something you do is of fear, dread, and/or obligation, you will not receive the true benefits you seek.

Do what you do in the moment because you authentically want to and love to, and not because you are afraid of what will happen if you don't. Be authentic and this will always bring you authentic results. Be aware of your motives and you will also be aware of the kind of experiences you are drawing forth and manifesting into your life.

Being aware means becoming attentive to the subconscious patterns and beliefs that are shaping your life automatically from beneath the surface. Subsequently, what you want is to align your subconscious beliefs with your purest intentions so that your conscious mind and subconscious mind work together in the fulfillment of your truest desires. What you need to do is become aware of your negative subconscious patterns, and then consciously transform them into patterns that work for you. Then you will have the best of both worlds; the conscious awareness that brings about appreciation and joy, and the automatic subconscious patterns that support you in your endeavors and in everything you manifest.

But being aware and contemplative moves beyond affecting what you manifest for yourself. It's also about being conscious of the needs of those around you, and knowing that you have the power to contribute to their joy as well. Don't get it wrong. It's not that you are responsible for the happiness of others, because each person makes their own choices about being happy. Rather, it's simply about knowing that everything you do has the potential to greatly benefit the lives of others in some way. It's as simple as knowing that you have the power to enlighten and uplift just by being your true self and sharing your joy.

So practice awareness everywhere you go. Take a look around you the next time you are on a bus, in a restaurant, or just walking down the street. Be aware of those around you. Know that we are all messengers for each other. Be conscious of people's needs and feelings too. Realize that your consciousness and your actions have an impact on others as well as yourself. Be present with what you're thinking, feeling, and doing, and use that knowledge to positively affect the world around you. Be a conscious participant in your life rather than a passive by-stander.

The simple truth is that we need to be more conscious of each other. Sure, sometimes we don't want to be bothered. Sometimes we are too involved in our own lives to notice anything or anyone else. But if you break out of your own bubble you'll suddenly notice how interconnected we really are.

Interconnection is not a burden; in fact it's liberating. It's taking comfort in knowing that we're all in this together. We are all of the same Energy Source, here to demonstrate peace, love, and creativity. We're all part of a bigger picture in which each of us plays a pivotal role. Understand that interconnection is not about taking the emotions or problems of others upon ourselves. It's simply about being aware of others and knowing that we each have something of value to share.

At the end of the day, contemplation, awareness, and overall presence are simply about being your true self. There is no greater gift that you can give to the world than to be authentic and to do what you came here to do. So use presence, awareness, and contemplation as tools to bring appreciation, purpose, and happiness back into your life.

APPLICATION:

To get you into a state of presence and awareness, start by slowing down, getting still, and noticing the types of thoughts and feelings you are experiencing in the moment. Assess your state of mind. Is what you are thinking, feeling, and doing aligned with your authenticity and joy? Or is it something that's taking you away from your right to be happy?

To illustrate how to use awareness and contemplation in your life, let's look at the concept of happiness. Happiness is an interesting topic, and a good one with which to start practicing your awareness and contemplative skills. The reason for this is because happiness, or the search for it, is what motivates us the most. So the more you understand what happiness means to you, and the more you are aware of its presence in your life, the more of it you will cultivate and experience.

When you lack happiness you create stress and struggle in your life. When you perceive everything from a lack mentality, no amount of money, things, people, or circumstances will ever be able to truly make you happy. Looking for happiness outside of yourself may provide you with some temporary relief or gratification, but if you are not happy from your core, you will always be chasing after happiness like a dog chasing after its own tail.

Put in simple terms, it is the desperate chase for happiness that ultimately causes stress in our lives. So stop chasing after happiness and start being it. Choose to be happy right now. Wherever you are in life, be aware of everything you have to be grateful for, right here and right now. Contemplate what happiness means to you personally. Does it come from having a new car? Does it come from being in a relationship? Does it come from your position at work? Realize that all these factors can certainly contribute to your happiness, but that without a strong core, your happiness will likely fluctuate as you move from one circumstance to another. If you want a more stable feeling of happiness, simply realize that your ability to be happy is already within you and is only a choice away.

Instead of being happy because of things and circumstances external to you, let those things and circumstances be representative of the happiness you already know is yours. Let them be reflections and manifestations of your truth, your purpose, your inner bliss, and your knowing that you are one with Infinite Abundance and Infinite Joy at all times. Then your happiness will not be dependent upon those things and circumstances, but you will be able to appreciate and enjoy them just the same. In fact, you will be able to appreciate and enjoy them even more knowing that they are positive expressions of the happiness already existing within you.

So what does happiness mean to you? What do you believe are the qualities that exemplify true happiness? Once you've determined your definition, embody those qualities as the essence of who you are right now.

For example, you could say that one quality of happiness involves having the freedom to express your passions in life. As such, you can choose to do so at any time. You can choose to release your fears and doubts, and instead, take one step forward in doing what you love. You can trust that it is your right to express yourself in this world, and even your purpose to do so, and then go ahead and take inspired action without any reservations. In this way, you will be living the essence of freedom in your life purely through the expression of your inner happiness and peace.

Become **aware** of the freedoms you already enjoy now. Focus on the feeling of freedom, and **contemplate** what that truly means to you. Then go out there and express this freedom in ways that are authentic to you. Express it, enjoy it, and share it.

Don't be fooled by false notions of happiness that come from your ego. Feel true happiness through appreciation and love, and even through your acceptance of the present moment. Know that as you appreciate life and feel happy from within, your happiness will not only show itself in your external circumstances, it will also be true, authentic, and consistently present in your life.

Contemplation and Awareness

So what about those times when you're not feeling so happy? Well, in those moments try to be conscious of what you think may be missing from your life. It's very important that you get to the root of your unhappiness or else you will likely project that unhappiness onto the world, which will simply throw it right back at you. If you mask the true reasons for your unhappiness you will also likely feed into one ego fix after another without ever feeling any real fulfillment at all.

So in order to get to the root of your unhappy state, ask yourself the following questions:

- "Why am I not happy right now? What is happening right now that is 'making' me feel unhappy?"
- "What perceived lack or void am I trying to fill in my life with something external to me?"
- "What do I really want? What qualities do I want to express that I am not currently expressing?"
- "Why do I want this? What is my motivation?"
- "What externally would need to happen in order for me to feel happy right now?"
- "Is there a way I can find this happiness within myself? What is the essence I am looking for and where can I find it in my life right now? How can I choose to express this essence right in this moment?"

If you go through this series of questions, and contemplate your answers, you will be able to pinpoint the truth of your dissatisfaction. And once you know where it's coming from, it will be that much easier to transform yourself into the naturally happy being that you came here to be.

Being aware of, contemplating, and understanding the root of your happiness, or unhappiness, is one of the most important things you can do. After all, everything we do comes from our desire to be happy and to express that happiness. Happiness is the biggest motivator there really is, so understanding its meaning is probably one of the most constructive things you can do. Know that no one has the power to make you happy or unhappy. You are the only one who can decide this, so be aware of this fact and you will be empowered to live a truly happy life, from the inside-out.

Each moment is a gift. Each moment is an opportunity to facilitate a life of joy and substance. So use each moment to its maximum potential; be present in it. Use contemplation and awareness to help you know yourself, and to appreciate and recognize each moment as the empowered gift that it is. Know that in doing so, you will be that much closer to living a life of peace, freedom, and total fulfillment.

Chapter 7:
Stillness

Look into a still body of water and you will not only see your reflection staring back at you, you will also see what lies beneath the surface.

Stillness can mean many things. It can imply a quieting of the mind, relaxation of the body, or a prolonged awareness of the present moment. Stillness is about relaxing the hectic pace of life, even if for a moment, but long enough to realize the truth that lies within.

Stillness is about being in the flow of things. It's about acceptance and existence. So many of us are so busy trying to get somewhere else, be someone else, or do something else that we forget who we truly are and what we truly want. We forget why we're doing what we're doing in the first place, i.e. what inspired it all. But when we accept who we are right now and where we are right now, we allow our true selves and our true joy to emerge. When we allow ourselves to be still for a moment, accepting the moment as it is without judgments or labels, we invite peace and guidance into our lives.

The past, the present, and the future make up the continuum of time and space as we know it. However, there is a place where all of these "times" come together as one, i.e. in the realm of consciousness. And it is within our consciousness that we can develop a keen awareness of the infinite possibilities we have available to us in every moment.

Stillness comes when we enter into this vortex where our limited concept of time and space simply doesn't exist. This vortex is the infinite place where all of our ideas are conceived and all of our desires and needs are energetically met before we even have them. It's a creative field where all thoughts, all potential, and all consciousness come together to form an infinite pool of possibilities. It's a place where all of your best possibilities await your acceptance of them.

So the lesson here is this: out of stillness comes creation. It's in stillness that you have the opportunity to look within and realize who you really are and what you truly want. It's a place where you can proactively connect with the truth of your being, your power, and your potential, and then transcend all of your perceived limitations.

Conventional meditation, for example, is something many people use to quiet their minds, relax their bodies, and connect with their higher-selves, yet there are some who have trouble getting to this place of stillness in this way. If you are one of those people, know that there are many ways of gaining similar results other than the conventional methods we often hear about.

In general, there really is no right or wrong way to meditate, so do not let the practice of meditation intimidate you. As long as it feels right to you and it's a method that allows you to bring your awareness into the present moment, then it's a good place to start. You can listen to music, take a walk in the park, exercise, or do whatever feels meditative to you. The only caveat is that you stay present with whatever you choose to do. Sure, it's great to remove yourself from all distractions and get Zen-like in your awareness, but if this is foreign to you know that you can really start anywhere with whatever feels right to you in the moment.

Meditation isn't rocket science, although sometimes it seems just that complicated. It's not something that needs to feel like a struggle. You cannot force yourself into a meditative state anyway. Actually, the more you try to force it, the harder it will be to get into it. It has to feel good to you. If it feels like a struggle you need to either choose another method, or change your perspective on the one you are currently using. Don't turn meditation into a task, a chore, or a results-driven activity. Let it flow naturally.

Don't be afraid to be still. Sometimes we fear stillness because it forces us to face ourselves and our fears. But this is the only way we will truly move past our self-imposed limitations; by being still enough to recognize the thought

Stillness

patterns that are causing us to limit ourselves in the first place.

When was the last time you took time to be still, with your thoughts, with your feelings, and with all that's going on around you? Many people fail to take advantage of this opportunity, but it is in this opportunity that peace resides. It is when you can still your worries, fears, and doubts that peace and joy and certainty can emerge.

Stillness is about feeling appreciation for what you have right now. It's about relaxing your mind and body long enough to feel the connection between you and the Infinite Universal Pool of all joyous possibilities. It's also about realizing which combinations and options from that infinite pool are truly best for you.

Stillness is about reconnecting with your higher-self and quieting the ego mind long enough to recognize the truth of your infinite nature. And when you get into this place of stillness, you are then able to find the flow of life that is devoid of stress and struggle and full of peace and happiness instead.

When you proactively get still, for even just a moment, you start to understand what freedom and peace truly feel like. You become fully engaged in the present moment, and as such, you allow all your worries and regrets to dissolve into nothingness. Stillness allows you to place everything into perspective, which then helps you make sense of yourself and your entire world. So take a moment now to get present and still and you will suddenly awaken to the abundance of knowledge, guidance, peace, and happiness you have available to you at all times.

APPLICATION:

To get yourself into the practice of stillness, start by taking at least 5-10 minutes each day to get quiet. Find a place where you can enjoy some privacy without being distracted. Now get comfortable, close your eyes, and allow your mind to be still. When thoughts pop up, gently brush them away. Visualize a white movie screen. As images arise simply move them off the screen. Keep your focus on stillness, on just being. Release all your worries, even for a moment, and allow your mind to be calm. Feel what it would feel like if you had absolutely no fears, worries, doubts, or insecurities. Feel what it would feel like to be totally relaxed, at peace, and completely fulfilled. In your stillness, dwell on the appreciation, joy, and peace you're experiencing right now.

If it's hard for you to clear and still your mind you can start by thinking about space, great bodies of water, or anything else that feels vast and infinite. Let your mind go, let your body relax, and let your spirit rise to the surface of your awareness. Feel your own infinite nature. Feel the oneness of your soul with everything and everyone. Feel your innate perfection. Now just sit with this feeling and let yourself be one with it.

Once you've been able to feel this stillness for a little while, notice if any inspirations come to you, like for instance, ideas, images, words, phrases, etc. Don't search for them and don't try to force them. Just be open to them. If they come, pay attention. If they don't, don't worry about it, just move on.

Also, if you have a question, now can be a good time to pose it, let it go, and allow the answer to come to you when the time is right. But a word of advice, pose your question always with the knowing that you already have the answer somewhere within you. This way you will not be coming at it from a perspective of lack, but rather a knowing that you already have access to everything you need to know right now. Know that since you are one with Universal Source Energy you already have all your answers within. And when you are able to still your mind, you help yourself welcome those answers; answers you were perhaps unable to previously recognize because of your scattered mind.

Once you are done meditating in this way, sit with the feeling of tranquility for a little while and then take it with you wherever you go. Infuse it into everything you do. Then you'll soon feel at peace and full of optimism in all areas of your life. And you will be amazed at what starts to manifest.

Furthermore, it's equally important to be able to cultivate feelings of tranquility and peace outside of meditation too. The true test is not just how you feel when you're alone in silence and comfort. The true test is out there; it's in how you react to the outside world. By cultivating an ability to maintain an inner tranquility, regardless of the circumstances around you, your awareness will become heightened to the point where you will be able to recognize your guidance when you receive it, and you will be able to tap into your intuitive powers, and subsequently, make your most proactive decisions.

So how do you cultivate this type of inner tranquility that can withstand external conditions? Practice. Practice being proactive rather than reactive. Practice compassion over anger. Practice pausing to contemplate your actions. Practice being aware. Ground yourself in the moment. Understand your motives, and always keep the truth in mind.

When you practice stillness, do your best to let go of all your worries and doubts, and then simply get into the space of unlimited potential. This is where all solutions and all answers reside. Every "problem" has its solution embedded within it. And just by allowing yourself to be in this space of unlimited possibilities brings those solutions to the surface of your conscious mind. Place yourself into this vortex of infinite possibilities by choosing to let go of your worries, and then let your infinite nature come to the surface of your awareness. Feel the freedom that this brings into your life.

Now, for some, the typical medium for meditation may feel foreign at first and so getting still can feel like a challenge. But remember, it's really about stilling your mind of worries and other blockages so that your truth can emerge. While this can happen in a typical meditative state, it can also happen in an active state if your mind is clear. So instead of getting discouraged, start your practice by engaging in an activity you enjoy and then make that your meditation. Get "still" with what you are doing. Meaning, take the time to really savor it, appreciate it, feel your connection to it, and ground yourself through it.

For instance, if you choose to go for a walk, notice how that feels, notice the sensations within your body, pay attention to what you are seeing and experiencing. Then just let go. Let go of your worries and instead focus on joy, love, and the grandness of The Universe. Marvel at the miracle of every creation, including you.

Once you get into the habit of getting still with your worries and over-consuming thoughts, and learn to appreciate each moment, you will allow flow and joy back into your life. And the more you get still and present with all that you do, the less stressed you will ultimately be, and the happier you will ultimately feel.

Chapter 8:
Enjoying the Moment

Enjoy the moment without worrying about the outcome and the outcome will joyously take care of itself.

Being present is about enjoying the moment as it is, without needing, chasing, or striving for more. It's about appreciating what you have right now. It's about releasing the need to know what's next and letting go of the chase for something bigger, better, or newer.

So many of us strive to get somewhere we think is better than where we are right now. We go from task to task, achievement to achievement, only to realize that we still want something more. Absolutely, desire, expansion, and growth are wonderful and necessary parts of life because they fuel creation, but we mustn't lose sight of each individual moment and the blessings that are encased within each one. If we spend our lives constantly running from one thing to another we will never fully appreciate or enjoy the joyous experiences that life has to offer us.

While we all have goals in our lives, it's best to approach these goals step by step, seeing each step as its own experience with its own merit. Look at each moment in your life as the goal in and of itself rather than just another stepping stone for getting somewhere else. Know that there is more to life than just getting somewhere else or getting something done. Life is about savoring joyous experiences and expressing passions. Life is about happiness and fulfillment. Life is meant to be enjoyed.

Stop thinking that the grass is greener over there somewhere. Stop chasing and start looking at what you have in your life right now. What blessings and opportunities are you allowing to pass you by in your incessant search for something "better"? What truth are you avoiding through your striving for something else? While sometimes a change in scenery can certainly be good, know that the common denominator is always you. As such, you can never run away from yourself.

So what's stopping you from enjoying yourself right now? Is your focus split? The fact is that we're often present in body but somewhere else in mind. As a result, we end up ignoring the present moment and what it has to offer. Think about it, how often do you find yourself already thinking about the next step before you've completed the one in front of you? You may have even dreamed about reaching this moment, but now that it has arrived, your focus has moved on to the next step, before you've even taken the time to enjoy where you are right now. You continue to robotically go through the motions not realizing that in doing so you're missing out on the full experience of the now.

Rather than jumping from one goal to another, enjoy each moment, be with it, then move on to the next goal, dream, or desire. But also realize that sometimes where you are and what you have right now is the goal you've been reaching for all along, only you're too involved in the chase to notice it. Know that constantly chasing after what you don't have will simply rob you of the full experience of enjoying what you do have. So instead, focus on what you do have and expand from there.

Understand that your focus in each moment is what essentially creates your future. So, the more prolonged your focus is on what you perceive you lack, the more frustration you will manifest into your life. But the more you focus on that which you love and enjoy, the more you will be carrying that feeling over into your future moments. So instead of focusing on what you feel you lack in your life, feel appreciation and joy in your heart for all that you have right here and right now.

Do not desperately chase after what you want, for if you do, you will be creating a stressful environment that will likely stunt your ability to cultivate the authentic happiness you desire. Instead, enjoy and appreciate each moment, as this will create a more peaceful environment in which your deepest desires will have the freedom to flourish.

Enjoying the moment is about creating a state of mind in which we can feel free to be authentic and do what we truly love. Unfortunately, many of us let fear stand in the way of us expressing our passions and purpose in life. But life is about enjoying each moment and living it to the fullest, not succumbing to fearful illusions. Awaken to what you love and then take inspired action in the moment that aligns with that. Just go for it, in spite of your insecurities. Then you will know what freedom is all about; freedom from fear and freedom from limitations.

To do what you love and to feel authentically good allows all else to fall into place naturally and joyously. So focus on what authentically feels good to you in each moment and you will come into your innate power to transform your life for the better. See each moment as an opportunity to notice something positive and to create an overall positive tone for your entire life.

Enjoying the moment means just that, enjoying the moment. Not waiting for something to happen in order for you to enjoy the moment. You do not have to wait for "perfection"; it's already within your reach, and already who you are at your core. Understand that if you are waiting for something to occur before you can actually enjoy the moment, you may end up always waiting for something and never truly being happy. If you wait for outer conditions to improve before you can allow yourself to feel happy, then even if they do improve, you'll likely find another reason to be unhappy. That's what happens when you depend solely on outer circumstances for your happiness.

Enjoying the moment and being authentically happy is really about understanding that you are one with Infinite Abundance and that you have access to it right now, and in every moment. You don't have to wait to feel the essence of your desires, to feel the essence of joy, peace, happiness, and the like, because you can access these feelings at any time, as liberally as you want to.

Enjoy each moment and make the most of it. Feel happy and whole now and you will be expressing your true state. Then your circumstances will rise up to match your positive attitude. Get rid of your "If/when _____ happens, then I'll be happy" mentality and find something to proactively enjoy and appreciate now, in the present moment. Then you will be aligned with who you truly are. Then you will be empowered to be authentically fulfilled.

Never feel guilty for enjoying your life and doing what you truly love from your soul. Know that you deserve to enjoy each moment and to live your life fully and joyously; it is your birthright. You simply need to align with that fact in order to start living a life of true fulfillment. Know that it is not selfish to feel authentically happy. If anything, it is from fullness that you have more to share with others. Know too that it's not about working hard for your happiness or justifying it to yourself or to others. It's about accepting your happiness and allowing it into your life because it is your right to have it, and it is yours already.

Enjoying each moment is about knowing that through your own personal joy you actually act as a positive example to others, inspiring them to be their best selves too. Know that being authentically happy benefits you, all those around you, and the world at large.

Some may wonder how they can possibly be happy in the face of so much struggle and pain going on in the world today. Well, here's the answer: you will not help anyone by being unhappy in your own life. No amount of your unhappiness will cause others to be happy. You cannot be sick enough to make anyone well. You cannot be poor enough to make anyone rich. The Universe just doesn't work that way, and the main reason for this is because the illusion of lack is just that, an illusion.

There is more than enough for all; you must believe in that if you are to help anyone. Understand that you cannot help anyone from a depleted standpoint. If you truly want to help others you must start with yourself, because when you feel whole and aligned with the truth, you have more to share with others. You can only give what you have to give, so make sure you fill yourself up with the truth of your infinite nature. Then enjoy each moment and be a beacon of light for all those in the world who need your personal brand of joy.

APPLICATION:

The more you can get into enjoying each moment of your life for its own sake, the more your life will be filled with peace, joy, love, and overall fulfillment. So start by choosing one activity a day to which you can fully commit yourself with enjoyment and present focus. Then, as you progress, expand your practice to enjoying more and more moments while you are in them. This way you will get into the habit of not only being present, but also making the most of your present moments, and hence, creating for yourself a higher quality of life.

Whatever you choose to do, do it with a light heart and a fun attitude. Refrain from thinking about what you have to do tomorrow, thinking about what you "should have" done yesterday, or worrying about outcomes. Spend this dedicated time solely on enjoying whatever it is you are choosing to do right now. Fully experience it. Focus on its positive aspects. Focus on appreciation. Remember, this is about choice, not obligation.

Understand that enjoying the moment is less about instant gratification and more about a prolonged appreciation for all that you have around you and within you already. So if/when you are feeling down and out, regroup and notice all that you have to be grateful for. This will automatically change your perspective, and subsequently, it will change the momentum of your life for the better, all because you chose to enjoy and appreciate the moment, and yourself, as is.

No glory comes from feeling guilty for enjoying your life. You deserve to be happy. So don't justify your joy. Don't excuse it. Don't rationalize it. Don't apologize for it. Just be it. Express your true self and the joy you feel in each moment, and as you do, you will be aligning yourself with more and more joy and success, which you can then share with others.

Enjoying the moment is about nurturing yourself from within. It's about seeing yourself as infinitely supplied with all that you need and love in every moment. It's about letting go and feeling free because you know that there's truly nothing to worry about. So use this perspective in all that you do and start enjoying yourself right now.

The more you can get into a mental state of infinite abundance and proactive gratitude, the more you'll be able to enjoy each moment because your mind and heart will be free from worry and stress. Think of yourself as a channel through which Eternal Love and Joyous Abundance infinitely flow. Think of yourself as a pipeline that is constantly circulating loving energy inward and outward. Know that you always have access to everything you need if you simply accept that as your truth.

It's important to emphasize here that in order to enjoy each moment you need to feel deserving and willing to do so. So take note of the excuses you use to avoid partaking in activities that you enjoy, excuses like, "I don't have the time," "I have other obligations," or "I have to be 'realistic.'" Notice your own self-sabotaging beliefs because these beliefs will stop you from enjoying your life to the fullest. Know that when you are happy and expressing your true self, others will benefit as well. Know that what's authentically good for you (and subsequently aligned with your purpose) must also be good for others, because we are all truly connected.

Truly loving yourself, being nurturing with yourself, and enjoying your life is not the same as being narcissistic, selfish, or self-indulgent. In truth, it all comes down to your intentions. Loving your ego is one thing. But authentically loving your true self and authentically enjoying your life are expressions of your appreciation for life itself and life's expression through you. It's an understanding that while it's important to love others as yourself, it's just as vital that you love yourself too so that you have love to share. Know that ego-love comes from insecurity, while loving your true self comes purely from appreciation. So ask yourself, "Where have I been using ego-love as overcompensation for my need for self-love?" "Where am I falling short on loving my true self?"

Know that loving your soul and enjoying yourself in each moment is about fully expressing your potential and the truth of your being. Then when you share with others you will be doing so from truth and authenticity. So practice being authentic in everything you do, do it from the heart, and enjoy every moment for the blessing that it is. Appreciate the moment at hand and know that it's a great opportunity to not only express your true self, but also share that self with the world.

Chapter 9:
The Journey is the Goal

In a way, life is like skydiving. The goal of skydiving is the journey. While the destination is important, the purpose of the ride is the ride.

Each of us has a unique purpose on this earth. Generally speaking, that purpose is to be totally happy and fulfilled and to share that fulfillment with others. Specifically speaking, when we choose to live our lives in an authentic way, our individualized purpose reveals itself to us and shows us the way to our personal fulfillment. Our core desires become clear and we are set on a joyous journey that benefits us and all those we touch.

Purpose is something that touches every part of your life. It influences you at your core and it guides you, that is, if you are willing to listen to what it has to say. It's saying that you are here to do great things, and that your journey is just as important as the destination itself. Your purpose is not just about the destination. Your purpose is infused into every step along the way, into every moment, and into every interaction.

When you make proactive choices that come from authenticity and joy, you align yourself with true fulfillment in all areas of your life. Your purpose is life itself, your experiences, and the choices you make. And every choice plays a pivotal role in the bigger picture of your life.

See your life as one great adventure. Rather than being afraid of the unknown, think of it as something fun and exciting. Transform your apprehension into enthusiasm. Think of your life as guided by a Divine Intelligence that wants to give you what you love. Trust that The Universe is looking out for you and providing for you based on your alignment with it.

Have wonderfully positive expectations without being concerned about or attached to a specific outcome or result.

When you view your life as a fun experience, you are then able to release the pressures associated with trying to be somewhere you think you "should be" that you're not. It's not a race and it's not a competition. Too many of us waste our time trying to do, or outdo, what others are doing, which only causes us to be inauthentic to ourselves; but we do not need to do that. Everyone has their own purpose and journey. Follow your own path. Be your best self.

Appreciate the experience of life itself. Consider the bigger picture. Release your judgments about what's "right" or "wrong," "good" or "bad," and just appreciate your life as an experience in and of itself. Realize what a gift it is. Realize how amazing it is to be able to experience different things, to love, laugh, observe, participate, etc. Sure you have your preferences, but the more you release your judgments and attachments, the less disappointed you'll be. And the more you learn to see the bigger picture of life, the more you'll realize how precious each moment truly is.

Don't be so serious. Have more fun. Laugh and love more. Even if things don't seem to be going your way, choose to see it all as a learning experience. Ask yourself if what you perceive as being dreadful is really all that important after all, or if it's just your ego pouting because it didn't get its way. Your journey is precious, so why waste a moment of it feeling sorry for yourself when you could be enjoying it instead. Go ahead, feel what you feel, express your emotions, but then realize that the choice to be happy and to enjoy your journey is totally up to you.

Think about how dynamic your journey is. Think about how empowered you are in each moment to create the life you want to live. All you need is to simply notice the feedback you're getting from life. Realize that your journey is the goal and that within this journey you are given infinite opportunities to live your life full of purpose and joy. Be proactive about how you choose to perceive your life experiences. In doing so you will become more empowered and more fulfilled than ever before.

The Journey is the Goal

See each moment as a new opportunity to create something great. This is your journey and each step has meaning. You must understand that your journey is about your overall purpose, and the steps along the way. Appreciate every step on your path, for each one has value, meaning, and opportunity embedded within it.

Nothing happens in vain. Everything that occurs does so for your benefit, to teach you something, and to express something. Be conscious of each moment. Be present with your experiences. Marvel at the ability you have to affect the tone of your life. Think about the miracle of creation and how you are one with it.

See your life as a glorious road trip with many destinations along the way. Know that there are many paths you can take, but that you're the only one who can choose which one feels right to you in any given moment.

You're on a path right now. This moment right now is already a destination in your life. Where you are right now is just as important as where you're going to next. And actually, where you are right now makes it possible for your next steps to even occur. One by one the chains of your journey link up, each one playing a vital role in the big picture of your life. So treat each moment as a joyous destination unto itself and you will not only get to where you want to be, you will also get there through joy, peace, and love. But most importantly, you'll realize that you're already there in spirit.

APPLICATION:

Think about a goal that you've already accomplished. Think back to all the steps leading up to that accomplishment, some you had foreseen and others that had brought you some surprises. Acknowledge the importance each step played in the fulfillment of your goal. Can you remember an occasion when the events in your life didn't make much sense, only to realize the full picture of it at a later time?

Now think of a goal you've set for yourself in the future. Think of some of the possible steps you may need to take to get you to your destination. Think about the significance each step will play in the bigger picture. Even though you may not know what each step along the way will be, realize how synchronized it all is and how each step plays its own role in the realization of your goals. Don't try to predict each step. Just be mindful of how connected each step is to your overall purpose. Recognize the significance that each step along your journey plays in the movie that is your life. Notice how everything is truly connected and synchronized.

Now, as you move forward in taking inspired action on your goal, be fully present and engaged with each step that you take. Take the time to enjoy it and let go of your need to know where it's going. Trust that with a strong intention to align with the truth, each step will take you on the journey you need to go. Be mindful of your choices and make your decisions with your consciousness in mind. Take the first step and trust that the next step will present itself when the time is right.

Release your judgments and attachments to how you think things "should be" because your perceptions could very well be skewed by your misinterpretation of the facts. Instead, see the significance of each step along your path and use it to learn something about yourself. Use the feedback you're getting (i.e. what you are seeing and experiencing in your life right now) to realize what you've drawn to yourself thus far, to notice what you've been focusing on the most, and to choose how you want your journey to continue. Then use your creative powers to make it so (i.e. realize you can be, do, and have the essence of anything you desire, and then align with and connect to that truth through your thoughts, feelings, beliefs, and actions).

Know that every journey starts with the first step. But also know that each step is pivotal to the one that follows it. Do not take your steps for granted. Savor each one and take in what it has to offer you.

Start practicing this awareness right now. What are you doing right now? What step in your journey are you taking right in this moment? Well, for one, you're reading this book so you are on the path of self-awareness and self-empowerment, which is a destination unto itself. Think of the effects this step might have on the rest of your life. Appreciate this moment as an important catalyst in the creation of the life you want to live. Now treat all your moments with this type of awareness and enthusiasm and you will create for yourself a beautiful life full of love, joy, and utter fulfillment.

Chapter 10:
Letting Go

Don't give up, just give it up. Surrender your path to guidance, to truth, to purpose, and you will find that your happiness has been with you all along.

What does it mean to let go? We hear about this concept all the time but sometimes it feels like it's easier said than done. Does letting go mean not caring? Does it mean being passive? Does it mean having no control?

Letting go simply means getting out of your own way by releasing your doubts and fears. When you try to control every aspect of your life what ends up happening is that you get attached to the way you think things "should" work out. If/when they don't work out as you had planned, you end up feeling depressed and disappointed as a result.

However, when you let go of all your attachments to the way you think things "should be," you allow your higher-self to guide you to what's actually best and most fulfilling for you. Being attached to the outcome and being desperate about it only causes you more stress and struggle. If you want to live your life with flow, peace, and joy, you must relinquish your need to control and to manipulate everything and everyone around you.

As such, letting go means being in the moment and allowing circumstances to be as they are right now. This by no means equals giving up. It simply allows you to release focus from what you don't want, and instead draw focus onto what you do want. It allows you to give up the desperation surrounding your desires, and to choose trust, faith, certainty, and patience instead.

When you obsess over something you don't want, you end up holding on to it with a tighter grip. When you obsess over something you do want, you end up pushing it farther away. Ironically, when you let go of your desperate need to change things as they are, you invite the changes you seek to occur naturally and easily.

Let go of your need to change people too. You are not here to force ideas onto anyone or to enforce what you think is right or wrong for them. Letting go means sharing your views and opinions without feeling the need for others to agree with you. It's about giving others the freedom to be who they are and who they want to be right now. It's about respecting everyone's right to follow their own path in life, without needing to judge them as right or wrong, good or bad. Accept people as they are and you'll be a lot more satisfied in your own relationships. If you try to change people, you will not only make yourself miserable, you'll also make others miserable in your attempts.

Always know, you cannot change anyone and it is never your job to do so anyway. People change when they choose to change and when they want to change. Love people unconditionally in each moment and accept them for who they are rather than trying to make them into someone you want them to be that they're not. You will be a lot happier this way.

When it comes to the circumstances in your life you must be willing to accept those as they are as well. When you accept things as they are, you simultaneously and automatically become a facilitator of change. Force and fight are never the best ways to change anything. We often think that the harder we fight against something, the faster things will change, but this is not necessarily so. The more you "fight against" something you don't like, the more resistance you create within yourself, and the more persistence you create with the very thing that you want to change. Focus on what you love. Let go of what you hate.

Our society, unfortunately, makes this difficult to do sometimes because we're so conditioned to think that fighting is good. Like "the fight against cancer," or "the fight against hunger," or "the fight against terrorism," etc. While the intention is certainly righteous, the focus is misaligned. Why not change the way we look at our causes and make them more about pro-action rather than reaction?

So then we can talk about movements that are "pro-health," "pro-sustenance," and "pro-peace." Feel how the change in perception triggers a change in how you feel in your heart. The former examples instigate a feeling of fear, resistance, and uncertainty, while the latter examples instigate a feeling of trust, joy, and confidence. Not fighting does not mean you've given up. It just means you've let go of your fear and instead embraced the truth. And from truth only good can come. So change the word "fight" to "proactivity." Then you will be able to keep your drive but let go of your desperation and fear.

Examine those times in your life when you felt you had conquered something. Was it the actual fight that did it, or was it your resolve, your hope, and your ability to let go of your fears? Even if it was "fight" that you were somewhat focused upon, perhaps your triumph could have come sooner and more easily if your focus was more proactive than reactive.

If each of us could just change our focus from problems to solutions and from unwanted conditions to joyous ones, we could finally eradicate disease, hunger, poverty, terrorism, and all those other negative conditions that have come out of the ego mind, once and for all. So start by letting go of the "fight," and continue by embracing love and joy and faith instead.

Letting go is about releasing your need to force what you want into existence. It's important to be ok with who and what and where you are right now, even if it's not where you think you "should be." Even if you don't like where you are, the only true way of changing it is by releasing your resistance to it. Once you do that, you will then be able to change your circumstances simply through your natural alignment with what you love. When you release your focus from what you don't like, you create a space that automatically fills itself with what you do like. It's as simple as that.

Let go of what no longer serves you, be it a relationship or a job or whatever the case may be. Learn from your experience and move on. Whatever it was, it served a purpose in your life, but if you hold on to it past its prime you will likely end up thwarting your progress. As such, you may end up blocking your next steps from arriving altogether. A situation in your life may have expired, but if you stay stuck on it you will not be present enough to recognize the opportunities that are being presented to you in the moment. So instead of lingering on a dead-end, move on with trust and faith and certainty in better things to come.

Again, letting go does not mean giving up. Letting go is about empowerment. It's about trusting that all is well, and then acting accordingly. It's simply about releasing your desperation so that you can allow your true self to emerge. And your true self is all about well-being in all respects. Let go of your hate, resentment, hurt, anger, betrayal, fear, doubt, insecurity, judgment, and the like, and embrace love, peace, joy, prosperity, confidence, and all good instead. Let go of your attachments and embrace what's truly best for you.

Letting go is about having faith in something bigger than yourself. It's trusting in an Infinite Energy that flows through you and to you and handles all of your affairs perfectly. It's about being open-minded and flexible. It's about looking beyond perceived obstacles and trusting that everything happens for a reason; that everything happens for your ultimate benefit, one way or another.

Letting go is about feeling free. Free from worry, free from disappointment, free from fear, and free from stress. Letting go is not about being passive. Actually, it's very proactive because when you let go you release your attachments to the outcome of your actions, and as a result, your actions become more likely to yield positive results. When you let go you allow yourself to come into your full potential because you are no longer wasting your moments focusing on anything negative.

We all desire to express the totality of our potential. As such, it's natural to feel frustrated if/when we don't feel like we're living up to that potential. But the answer is not to push harder. The answer lies in letting go. If you push harder you will be swimming against the stream rather than with the natural current of life. So let go of the "shoulds" in your life and instead embrace the truth of who you are. Instead of focusing on what you "should be doing," focus on what "you'd like to be doing" instead. This will release the pressure and align you with the guidance and flow that is available to you at all times, which will then naturally lead you to experience the life you truly desire.

Now, if you are feeling frustrated with the way your life is generally going you can use this as a sign that you are ready for a positive change; that you are ready to embrace your true destiny of infinite potential by letting go of your false beliefs. Do not dwell on disappointment. Do not attach yourself to specifics. Just trust that you have it in you to be happy and fulfilled right now. Just trust that you are capable of greatness, and then go be great. This may appear impossible to do in the moment, but it truly is as simple as making the choice to do so, in your mind and in your heart.

Letting go is about releasing negative patterns and stagnant beliefs. It's about using the feedback you get from your life as a vehicle for change where change is needed. It's about being more empowered by releasing your fears and insecurities so that your happiness is no longer dependant on everything external to you. Listen to your life, it's talking to you. The more you ignore its calls, the more struggle you will likely endure.

Letting go means allowing "what is" to be what it is, and in doing so, being open to feedback. It means releasing your need to predict the future and releasing your regrets of the past. It means being open and faithful and choosing your focus consciously. When you learn to let go of your fears, your doubts, and your attachments, you will learn what freedom is all about. When you can experience each moment for its own sake, without needing it to be something else, you will be free to appreciate the opportunities and guidance that are being presented to you right now. You will be able to embrace the lessons, the joys, the blessings, the synchronicities, all the while being mindful of the bigger picture.

When you appreciate life for the sake of its own experience your perspective changes and you become better able to focus on love, joy, peace, and all things good. With that said, it can sometimes seem difficult to focus on the good of the present moment, to let go of all your fears and doubts when you are experiencing something you don't particularly like. But what's the alternative? Staying stuck in fear? Wouldn't letting go feel so much more liberating? It may gratify your ego to dwell on your fears and to prepare yourself for the worst, but this is not a practical approach. If you understand that your thoughts shape your reality, it just doesn't make sense to dwell on the undesirable.

So stop in the moment and think about the miracle and blessing of life itself, stop to consider the bigger picture. Then you will be able to shift your attitude from a negative one to one of appreciation. And from appreciation your experience will naturally become uplifted to exemplify that which you love and that which authentically feels good to you.

Never underestimate the power within your present moments. The perceptions you choose now will create the tone of your experiences to come. So choose to let go of what doesn't feel good, choose to let go of negative expectations, and choose to let go of your need to know everything right now. Just trust in Divine Order, Divine Wisdom, and in your personal power. Know that the essence of anything you desire is not only possible, but already yours to receive. Know that the more you let go and start enjoying each moment of your life, to any degree whatsoever, the more you'll be aligned with what you love. And the more aligned you are with what you love, the more joy you will manifest into your life.

Everything in your life is there for your benefit. It may not appear as such in the moment, but when you let go of your fears, insecurities, defensiveness, and worries you will notice the lessons you need to learn, and the guidance you're getting on what to do next. Any unwanted condition is ultimately a result of something from within you; a misalignment of sorts from the truth of All There Is. As within so without. So the more you can accept yourself and the moment as it is, the clearer you'll be on the original cause of your circumstances. But you must be willing to take responsibility, and you can only do that when you've let go of your self-pity and concern over what's to come.

Letting Go

Letting go means having patience. When you are patient you are free to enjoy and simply appreciate the moment as it is, without feeling the need to rush into anything else. Rushing creates stress. Chasing and striving create stress. Letting go into the moment brings peace back into your life.

So let go of your need to know how, when, and where your desires will manifest. All this is truly the domain of The Universe anyway. All you need to know is who you are at your core, align with your purpose, and act out of inspiration, integrity, authenticity, and joy.

Now it's understandable to want something better to occur if/when you are experiencing something you don't particularly like or want. But the ironic thing is that wanting it and chasing after it and trying to push it and feeling desperate about it, while it all feels like the natural response, is actually the worst thing you can do. You want what you want when you want it. But in order to get it you need to let go of your desperation for it. Yes, it can seem hard to do this, but the more faith and patience you have, the easier it will be. And once you get to that place of genuine surrender, you'll be amazed at how quickly you will feel at peace and how quickly you'll start to see things shift for the better.

When you are patient you do not feel the need to push, force, strive, manipulate, or chase after anything. Instead, you are able to let go of your intentions, which in turn, allows you to manifest your heart's desires with ease and joy. The secret is this: when you are no longer worried or agonizing over what you want, then what you want, or something even better, is free to come to you with ease, and often in pleasantly surprising ways.

Practice patience and letting go with all of your genuine desires and watch as things miraculously unfold. Simply be present with where you are. You can have your goals, intentions, and desires in mind, just allow them the freedom to materialize when and as they may. Learn to let go of your desperation and you will find that what you've been chasing after suddenly starts chasing after you.

You Are Here

Letting go means trusting in the process of life, being a conscious participant, and simply enjoying the ride. It means refusing to desperately pursue or keep score. It means doing what's most authentic to you in each moment and trusting that this will always bring you total fulfillment and true happiness. So let go of your need to control, and relax into the joy you are meant to experience, right here, right now, and always.

APPLICATION:

Think of something you really want. How do you feel about it? Does it inspire thoughts and feelings of joy and enthusiasm within you, or does it bring up feelings of doubt and impatience? Are you feeling desperate or attached about having it?

If you are feeling attached to the outcome of something specific, focus instead on the essence you want to experience. For example, say you want a promotion at work, instead of being fixated on a specific position, focus on the feelings you are looking to cultivate from having that position. This can be the essence of security, joy, creative expression, satisfaction, fulfillment, purpose, etc.

Then focus on where in your current position you can cultivate these same essence feelings, because the more you focus on having that essence, the more that essence will be drawn to you in other ways too. So, for instance, focus on the security and appreciation you feel from having the job you have right now. Focus on putting your all into the tasks you have at your current position and making the most of your talents there. As a result, soon you will see things shift for the better, starting with your perceptions and then overflowing into your outer circumstances.

If you're out of work, focus on the essence of freedom that you have to explore yourself and your desires. Focus on the time you have to develop your goals, skills, and your resilience. And the same goes with other desires like wanting an improved physical condition or desiring a loving relationship. No matter what it is that you want, focus on the essence you believe it will provide for you and feel this essence in your life right now.

Once you've pinpointed the essence that you want to express, let go of any attachment you may have to your personal timeline, as well as the need to know how it will all come together. Just trust in this essence as being who you are already, and know that the more you embrace this essence as your truth now, the faster it will show up in your life in physical form and experience too.

Some of us have a hard time understanding the concept that we already have everything we need within us. That's why we tend to focus on the external so much. But if you understand the concept of energy, and the fact that we are all made up of it (as is everything else), you'll understand that you are already one with everything you could ever desire. You are one with it through your energetic connection to it. It is you, you are it. Whatever you want to manifest into your life is already an essence that is within you to express. And so, when you align with this truth, even simply through your acknowledgment of it, you start to manifest that essence into your life.

So now, to get further into the essence feeling of what you love and want to express, envision what that expression might look like. Paint a picture of it in your mind; just be sure not to get attached to anything too specific. Instead, use these details to further perpetuate your essence experience. So, for example, if your focus is on the essence of job satisfaction, envision yourself being and doing what you love. Feel yourself in that role. What does that feel like to you? Or if you want to be healthier, fit, more abundant, in a healthy relationship, or whatever the case may be, feel what that would feel like. What does it look like in your mind's eye?

Then, notice how the essence you seek is already present in your life right now. Notice it in your surroundings. Notice it in your memories of previous experiences. Even notice it in the successes of other people, and be happy for them. Notice it right now in whatever ways it's expressing itself in your life. Notice it simply as an expression of truth; the truth that you already have everything you need and desire within you. No matter how little you think you have going for you, find something you can appreciate right now. Don't be jealous of others. Instead, use what you see around you to inspire you, and then see it as a sign of good things to come. Don't focus on what others have that you don't. Focus on what you have and appreciate every bit of it. Feel the essence you want to express and then let go.

Trust that as you let go of your attachments you will be drawing more of the essence you love into your life. Trust that what is best is always manifesting for you, and know that if the specifics that manifest are not exactly as you thought, there's a good reason for it (i.e. it's either showing you where you need to align, or it's telling you that there's something even better for you). And you'll know what that reason is by being present and aware of how you're feeling in the moment. If you are feeling desperate and attached, then you can bet that the feedback you're getting is showing you what you need to adjust. But if you are feeling aligned and at peace, you'll know that you are attracting what's best and most fulfilling for you.

As long as you are aligned with your inner truth, and you are not attached to any specific outcome, practicing this detached way of thinking will progressively release you from stress, and allow you to joyously live the life you've always wanted, and perhaps even better.

Let go of your need to change "what is." Know that letting go of your need for things to be different doesn't mean you've conceded to things staying the same. It simply means you are no longer worried about it. When you let go of your need to change things, what you are giving up is not necessarily the desire to change things, but rather the desperation to change things. Desperation indicates lack, and lack attracts more lack. Letting go and accepting things as they are is really about trusting that your true state is one of total well-being. And the more you align with this truth, the faster it will manifest into your experience.

If there is something in your life you would like to change for the better, start by releasing your resistance to it. Let go of your need for things to be different and you will find that your focus will naturally gravitate towards positivity. Once you let go of your resistance, what you actually desire to express will manifest with greater ease.

Whether you are experiencing a health issue, financial issue, relationship issue, or whatever it is you are struggling with at this time, release your focus from what you want to change, and embrace what you want to experience and express instead. So rather than focusing on getting out of debt, focus on being joyously wealthy and financially free. Instead of focusing on getting out of a bad relationship, focus on being in a good one. Instead of focusing on fighting a cold, focus on being healthy. Align yourself with positive thoughts, feelings, beliefs, and actions and be patient and loving with yourself. The faster you can release your resistance, the sooner you will see positive changes occurring in your life.

Understand that giving up the chase is really about giving up your desperation and your despair. It's about being content in the moment because you know that you are whole as you are. It's about being optimistic of things to come, but in their own time and in their own way.

Below you will find an affirmation you can use that will help you let go of any attachments you might have to outcome, as well as express your faith and trust in the process of life.

First, think of something you desire, something that you love to do, something that feels authentically good to you. Then affirm the following:

> "I trust that somehow the essence of my authentic desire is manifesting always in the best ways. I let go of my own agendas, my impatience, and my need to rush the process. I trust that all is working out well and I know that it's all happening in the perfect time and order for me. I already have everything I need and could ever want within me right now to express, and this truth is being joyously displayed in every moment of my life. I relax my need to know when and how my desire will manifest as I allow my highest good to come forth in each moment in perfect ways. I humbly allow myself to be the perfect channel through which Source Energy flows, and I trust that this will always fulfill me in the best of ways."

What an affirmation like this can do is help you shift your perceptions. And shifting your perceptions is one of the quickest ways to change anything you want to change. So shift your perceptions from lack to abundance, from hate to love, from stress to ease, and so on.

Letting go and changing your perceptions can also help you release your frustrations when things don't seem to be going your way. For instance, if you are ever feeling overwhelmed or stuck, by changing your focus you can free your mind to become better aware of a solution. Just leave what you are doing for the moment and go do something else. Letting go in this way will allow you to be open to receiving exactly what you need. Shifting your present awareness onto something that feels better frees you of worry, and as such, frees your mind to come up with the answers you seek, without stress or struggle.

Worry is another way of creating stress in your life. So let go of your worries, about yourself, about what's to be, and about others too. When you worry you are not really helping anyone anyway. You are only placing more of your focus onto something you don't like and don't want. Choose instead to expect the best, let go, and trust The Universe to deliver what's best for all.

Use the power of letting go whenever you feel attached to something, worried about something, or in search of an answer. Free yourself from all that bothers you. Feel the essence of everything being taken care of for you effortlessly and joyously. Trust that as your faith grows, so will your ability to let go. Before you know it you will feel more at peace, more centered, more joyous, and more fulfilled than you ever thought was possible.

Stop Struggling:
If you feel something is too much of a struggle and you're trying too hard to force it to be the way you think it "should be," or how you want it to be, then stop. If something is truly right for you it won't feel like a struggle. It may take some effort, but the effort will feel joyous, not torturous. Struggle comes from your own resistance. But if you are in the flow you won't feel this resistance.

Struggle shows you where you are off your path and where you are not aligned. You can continue to push and force and manipulate to get what you want, or you can choose to see what this struggle is trying to show you. For instance, where are you closing yourself off from flow and guidance? Where are you attached to outcome? What ego gratification are you seeking? Struggle comes from not being able to let go, but it also comes from chasing after the whims of your ego. To counter that, understand why you want what you want in the first place, and realize that what you think you want may very well be different from what you actually want.

No matter what you desire, to save yourself time and struggle, just be clear with yourself about your actual motivation. It may be ego-driven or it may be soul-inspired. The key is to simply be aware of why you do what you do and why you want what you want. Then you will know what you really desire and whether or not it's worth pursuing. Then you'll be able to properly direct your focus onto what you actually desire and what's most proactive, rather than your ego's desires, which aren't real anyway.

Let The Universe carry you to where you need to be. Relinquish your need to control your circumstances or manipulate them to be a certain way, and just trust that "what is," is best, right now. Then let go and let The Flow carry you.

Chapter 11:
Acceptance and Allowing

Believe that your life is right, right now. Trust that everything has its reason, and just go with it, knowing that it will all come together in due time.

Accepting things as they are right now allows you to give up the desperate chase for what you want, which then releases resistance within you, and subsequently, allows what's truly best for you to unfold. But know that giving up the chase and accepting things as they are isn't about losing hope. Rather, it's about gaining perspective and opening yourself up to the best outcomes for you.

When we are unable to accept our lives as they are, and ourselves as we are, we become panicky and disheartened. We convince ourselves that if we were richer, prettier, taller, thinner, smarter, or whatever the case may be, that we would be happier and more worthy of love. But this type of chasing only makes us feel worse about ourselves and more stressed out.

To accept yourself in the present is to accept the blessing that you are to the world. Think about it. There is no one else out there exactly like you, with your exact qualities, with your exact purpose. Why would you want to devalue that by rejecting who you are?

Grow into the person you are meant to be, and everything you love will come to you naturally. But it all starts with acceptance, because without acceptance you can never fully appreciate who you are or what you have. And as such, you will fail to allow yourself to fully come into your own because you will be too fixated on what you think you lack.

Understand that the key to releasing stress and frustration from your life and to living a life of joy and fulfillment is to simply accept "what is" without feeling the need to judge it or label it. It's about being happy in the moment so that you can expand on that happiness as you move forward in life. Understand that being happy and accepting of your life right now does not prevent you from being, doing, and/or having more. In fact, it supports your expansion; only it does so from a perspective of truth and wholeness rather than ego and lack. Meaning, when you are happy and accepting of the present moment you allow more of that happiness to flow to you.

While accepting "what is" can sometimes feel challenging to do, it becomes easier when you realize and understand that there is a reason and purpose for everything in your life. In this moment something may seem "bad" to you, but in the bigger picture it can serve a higher purpose that will ultimately lead to your joy and fulfillment. So don't be so quick to negatively judge your present circumstances. Just because you aren't aware of the outcome yet doesn't mean you won't ultimately like it. Trust that whatever is going on in your life right now is in one way or another preparing you for things to come. Trust that it is showing you what you need to see.

So pay attention, release your judgments, align with your true self, and watch as your life's events miraculously unfold. Trust that the more aligned you are with your truth, the more things will make sense to you. Your significant other broke up with you? Accept it as an opening to know yourself better and to attract a better match. Lose your job? Accept it as an opportunity to launch your passion and follow your dream. Even an ailment can show you where you have been energetically blocking yourself for days, weeks, or even years prior. Perception is everything so choose yours wisely.

Perceive the challenges or obstacles in your life, or what you have labeled as such, as opportunities for growth, learning, and transformation. Challenges are simply there to show you where you have become misaligned with your truth. If you look at them with acceptance you will allow yourself to grow from them, and as a result, choose better options for your future.

We all come here to learn certain things, mainly the understanding of

Acceptance and Allowing

who we are, where we come from, and the scope of our power. We are here to express, experience, and share. Subsequently, when we choose to align with our truth, versus our ego, we also allow ourselves to learn things proactively versus reactively. Think about it, wouldn't you prefer to learn through inspiration and guidance rather than trials and tribulation? Well, aligning with your truth leaves you open to guidance from Universal Wisdom, which then allows you to receive lessons in more proactive and peaceful ways; no wake-up calls necessary.

When you are accepting of things as they are, what you are doing is empowering yourself to transform your life for the better. Acceptance does not mean defeat, nor does it mean accepting your current circumstances as your eternal fate. It simply means releasing resistance to what you don't want, taking responsibility for your mindset, realizing that within this very moment exists an opportunity for greatness, and then choosing to act upon this opportunity.

Understand that by resisting something you are only giving it more power. If you resist, worry over, fight against, or dwell upon something you dislike, you are only giving it more of your attention. But by accepting "what is," you are freeing yourself up to move on by allowing a new and better attitude, belief, and focus to emerge. And when your mind is free from worry you're left with a vacuum that must fill itself, and if you're not focused on the negative, you're only left with the positive.

So instead of focusing on what you do not enjoy, feel how it would feel to be, do, and have that which you do love and enjoy; feel it as your reality right now. The more you focus on what you authentically desire and love, and feel it in the moment, the more you will be aligned with your true self, and the more you will magnetize and allow that essence into your life.

When you accept "what is" you allow the flow of life to guide you. Conversely, when you fight against something you do not like or want, you create a counter-force that only makes positive change more difficult to attain. When you accept and allow things to be as they are, without jumping to judgments or placing labels, you release negative focus, thus freeing yourself up for a shift in consciousness, and subsequently in experience too.

In order to shift your consciousness, however, you must learn to no longer deny how you truly feel. Sometimes we put on a brave face or try to be overly optimistic, hoping that something will change as a result. We affirm what we want over and over, all the while feeling doubtful and resentful of where we actually are. But if your optimism is not authentic it can cause even more resistance within you. So instead of denying or sweeping your feelings under the rug, be honest about how you truly feel, versus how you think you're "supposed to" feel. Don't put on a show for others or for yourself. Just be real, be true, be you.

Acceptance has to be real. You cannot repress an emotion and call it acceptance. Repression is the opposite of acceptance. In fact, it is a form of denial. Denying how you truly feel will not solve anything. When you repress your feelings and thoughts you create more resistance within you. As a result, that which is being repressed ends up lingering in your subconscious mind until it is dealt with, if it's dealt with at all.

So instead of repressing your true feelings, feel what you feel and accept it without judging yourself for what you are feeling. It is better to feel it, express it (as proactively as possible), deal with it, and then let it go, than it is to keep it packed up tightly, ready to explode at a moment's notice. Repression fuels the negative subconscious beliefs that keep you from fulfilling your deepest desires. Consequently, only when you have accepted and dealt with your true emotions can you truly move on peacefully.

Many people, especially those who are enlightened to the power of positive thinking, are often afraid to accept and feel negative emotions. They think that by doing so they will attract the very essence of what they are feeling. However, when you repress your true feelings, this is exactly what happens; your negative focus becomes prolonged within your subconscious mind, and this carries over into your thoughts, feelings, beliefs, actions, and experiences too. So don't be afraid to face your fears and true emotions. As long as your overall momentum is positive, you're still on track.

Acceptance and Allowing

Understand that by not accepting your feelings in the moment you are actually working on creating exactly what you fear. As such, you mustn't lose sight of the importance of recognizing and dealing with your true feelings in the moment before they get too out of control and start manifesting themselves in your physical world.

Do not dwell on your negative emotions. Just recognize that they are there, and then get to the root, the thought patterns, and the belief systems that have been causing these feelings within you. This isn't about exhaustively psycho-analyzing yourself. It's about being honest about what you truly believe, because when you are aware of your beliefs and true feelings you can then successfully uproot what isn't working for you. You can genuinely feel good feelings and think good thoughts without the threat of negativity lurking under the surface, waiting to undermine your intentions.

So notice now if you have any negative beliefs or negative feelings that you've been denying or suppressing. Notice if you've been spending more time fighting, defending, or rejecting than you have been accepting, allowing, and dealing.

Know that when you fight against something you only feed into it more. So ask yourself, is there something in your life that you've been fighting against? As you've done so, have you found your life's circumstances getting better or worse?

If you've found that the circumstances in your life have not been getting better, chances are it's due to all the resistance you've been creating through your focus on what you don't like or want, or your repression of it. Understand that when you focus on what you lack you attract more lack. And when you repress how you truly feel, you strengthen your negative subconscious beliefs, and again, attract more lack.

The formula is quite simple. Be honest about how you feel and you will be empowered to manifest the life you love. If you are not seeing the results you seek, notice where you may be resisting what's going on in your life right now, or where you may be repressing how you truly feel about your ability to have what you desire.

Think about each area of your life. Is there something that you authentically desire that you've had trouble attracting thus far? Notice how you feel about it. Are you desperate about it or relaxed? If you're desperate, most likely you are not getting the results you seek because you perceive a lack of what you desire in your life right now, and as such, you are not aligned with it. Or perhaps the timing just isn't right yet but out of impatience you have come to feel despaired about it. Maybe you are longing for what might have been. Or perhaps you are fantasizing about the future and how "someday" things will be better. Your "someday" may come, but it will come when you release your resistance to "what is," and when you embrace the essence (the feeling) of having what you love right now. Then your "someday" will become "today."

Acceptance means being present with where you are right now and being ok with it because you know the truth of who you are at your core. It's about keeping a positive perspective and not allowing your present circumstances to necessarily define who you are, or determine what is or isn't possible for you. It's about trusting in Divine Timing and Order as you go about your business of aligning with the true you.

Acceptance is about knowing that what is right for you is right for you and will manifest in its own time. It's understanding that the more aligned you are with your true self, the less resistance or interference you will be creating with respect to the manifestation of what you truly love.

Acceptance is about taking responsibility. It's about knowing that you are a powerhouse of energy that attracts into your life the essence on which you focus the most. So realize how powerful you really are and use your focus purposefully to shift your consciousness, your habitual thinking, your actions, and subsequently, your entire life experience for the better.

Accept yourself for who you are right now because you are exactly where you need to be for your unique purpose. How you come into this world is a matter of purpose, and what you do while you're here is also a matter of choice. Whether you align with your purpose and truth or not is totally up to you.

Acceptance and Allowing

If you don't like what you see, use it as feedback to stimulate change. Every moment has its blessing, whether obvious or not. Know that nothing ever happens by accident so use your present moments as guidance to show you where you might be out of synch with the truth of who you are, and with the essence of what you want to express.

Realize your true value and you will create for yourself the life you've always dreamed of. If you deny or fight against your present moments, however, and if you spend your life constantly trying to prove something to others, rather than being true to yourself, you will likely create more stress, struggle, and frustration as a result.

Love yourself. Accept yourself. Know that you are enough right now. Your soul is always enough. You do not have to prove anything to anyone. You can be free and true to yourself without making justifications or excuses for it. You can accept where you are right now, and you can choose to direct your focus onto alignment with your true self. Once you realize that you are already good enough as you are, you will naturally release the need to people-please or prove that you are good enough to anyone.

Do not allow your past experiences, others' opinions of you, or your own fears to run your show. Know that each moment is a unique opportunity to allow something great into your life. If you allow your fears to control you, however, you will miss out on the beauty that's right in front of you.

When you get present and accepting you will suddenly realize that what happened in the past does not need to determine what's to come, and that what other people think does not need to influence your outcomes or your opinion of yourself. You will likely realize that what you fear is simply an illusion, and that you can choose to align with the truth at any time. And the truth is that at your core you are already perfect and whole in your own unique way, and that you have the power within you to draw forth to you the life you love. That it is through your acceptance of your true self, and the subsequent actions you take that align with that self, that you will manifest what you truly love.

Understand that accepting "what is" means observing it rather than reacting to it. If you can be objective about it and non-resistant to it you will open yourself up to allowing your true well-being to come forth in all areas of your life. It's like fear, if you face it head on, or you are at least willing to do so, you will often realize that there was nothing to fear in the first place. When you are willing to face your fears, those fears disappear. As such, when you are willing to accept "what is," you enable yourself to switch focus, and subsequently, open yourself up for transformation.

Transformation, although it may seem like an intimidating term, is actually simply a matter of acceptance and moving on. It's a process of shifting your focus onto the reality of your choosing rather than limiting yourself with negative perceptions. Transformation is not about becoming someone you're not. It's about becoming your true self beyond the negative influences of your ego. So be the person you want to be right now and embody the life you want to live right now, despite outer appearances. Trust that the appearances in your life will align to match your internal reality. Focus on your alignment with the truth of who you really are, and the rest will follow suit. And know that you can jump into the essence you desire at any time.

Your true state is one of perfection, even if you aren't aware of it right now. You must have faith in this truth and not allow outward appearances to cloud your judgment. Know that all your quirks and all your traits make up the sum of your perfect self. Everything you're here to learn and everything you're here to do, it all makes up the unique person that you are. Your perfection does not come from some artificial standard or ideal. It comes from your acceptance of your true self and your willingness to move beyond your ego. It comes from your ability to feel and be the essence of who you want to be right now because you know it's who you are already. You do not need to stay stuck in your self-imposed limitations. Instead, you can choose to come into your authenticity right now, one moment and one action at a time.

When you stop interfering with your true nature, you automatically allow your true happiness to emerge. When you are able to use your present

Acceptance and Allowing

moments to create positive intentions, and follow-through on them, you allow everything else to fall joyously into place, without force or fight. The Universe knows what to do. So allow yourself to receive its bounty by simply accepting yourself, aligning yourself with the truth, and acting in accordance with that truth.

APPLICATION:

Think of something you've been fighting against for some time. Whatever it is, recognize the resistance you've been causing within yourself by your focus on it. Once you've pinpointed an area where you know you have been resisting something, be willing to let it go. Feel the feeling so as not to repress it, but then let go of it. Know that there is a lesson here and a reason for everything. See each moment as an opportunity to release what isn't working for you, and to embrace what will instead.

Affirm: "If this is what needs to be right now then so be it. It is what it is. I surrender and trust The Universe to bring me what I love, but I also accept the moment as it is and take full responsibility for it. I can always choose what I love and manifest it, and so it is. I am ready to accept and receive what I love with joy and proactive gratitude. Thank you."

It's important that you look at each step in your life as an adventure. Be excited to see where it's leading you rather than dreading it every step of the way. Look at it as objectively as you can. Take on a positive attitude, even if you don't know specifically what the outcome will be. For example, if something doesn't seem to be going the way you'd like, take on the attitude of, "Hmm, this is interesting. I know there's a good reason for this. I'll look at it as an opportunity. Even if I don't yet know what the outcome will be, I trust that it will all work out great. I'll just focus on what I can do to help my progress along and then let go of the rest." This is the epitome of having positive expectations, taking responsibility, while also allowing and accepting things as they are.

Understand that your attitude, focus, feelings, and actions combined will bring you matching results in your external world. Like it or not, that's how the laws of The Universe work. It makes logical sense then to take the optimistic route where you trust that everything always works out for the best. It's simply the most efficient, effective, and pragmatic stance to take because not only does it release your focus from what you want to change (i.e. that which you don't like), it also subsequently allows what you want to experience (i.e. that which you do like) to manifest.

Acceptance and Allowing

It's important that you maintain a positive attitude as your general way of being because this automatically releases resistance from you. However, repressing your feelings won't work. So give yourself permission to feel whatever it is you are feeling without feeling guilty for it. Just know when you've crossed the line between productive expression and self-destruction. Be sure that your positivity and optimism are authentic. You cannot fake-out The Universe. Your feelings are what truly count. So make sure your subconscious environment (i.e. your beliefs, feelings, and thoughts) matches your conscious intentions and actions.

As it turns out, being present allows you to better understand your subconscious environment in that it makes you aware of the possible underlying causes that are behind your unwanted conditions. However, when you are not present and aware, sometimes it's difficult to know how you truly feel about something. As such, you may think you are aligned with what you want when in actuality you might not be. As such, you could end up wasting days, months, and even years of your life wondering why things are not working out for you.

So, to make sure you are not repressing any negative beliefs, think about what you want to experience in your life. What feelings come up? You may find that fearful thoughts of doubt and insecurity emerge, or perhaps a deep-rooted belief that you've adopted from others around you. Noticing how you feel when you think about your deepest desires will show you where you may be holding resistance. And when you become aware of your resistance, you can then let it go.

When you become aware of your feelings and true beliefs you become more accepting of yourself and of your present moments. Accepting yourself simply means understanding that you are already whole and complete as you are. It's knowing that the negative patterns that have caused you to misalign with the truth stem from illusions and figments of your ego's imagination. When you can accept yourself for who you are and where you are, you will finally find the freedom and ultimate joy that you seek. You will be able to see the errors in your thinking, and through this awareness, you will naturally release whatever does not fulfill you, thus allowing what does fulfill you to naturally surface.

Use this affirmation when you need a reminder to accept yourself and the present moment as it is:

> "I accept myself as I am right now. I am exactly where I need to be for my personal journey. How I perceive my life is up to me, so I choose joy, happiness, and peace, right here, right now, and always."

The fastest way to get to living the life you love is to accept where you are right now, because in doing so, you will be allowing the truth of your being to emerge. Everyone starts somewhere; your somewhere is right here and right now. Every moment is a new opportunity to create something wonderful. Use it to its maximum potential. Don't waste it on resisting the present moment or wallowing in your regrets.

Surrender your desires to The Universe. Have patience and trust in Divine Order. Let go of your need to micromanage every detail of your life. Take inspired action, but then surrender your needs, your fears, and your attachments, and allow your wonderful and joyous destiny of total fulfillment to naturally unfold before you.

Chapter 12:

Releasing Fear and Dumping Regret

What was, was. What will be, will be. But what is controls it all.

Fear and regret are probably the two most destructive emotions anyone can experience for they can cause all sorts of obstacles and challenges that simply do not serve anyone well. The key isn't to feel embarrassed or be ashamed of your fears. Rather, it's to acknowledge how false your fears really are. As such, when you are present you are able to release your fears and let go of your regrets simply because presence brings perspective back into your life.

You are always here and now. Your mind may wander off to tomorrow or reminisce about yesterday, but truly you are only ever in the now, feeling what you are feeling in the now, and doing what you are doing in the now. Even as you are thinking about the past or the future, you are thinking about it in the now. So it would make sense then to pay attention to the now and actively choose what you do with your present moments.

When you wander off from the present sometimes your fears can get the best of you. Actually, a lot of your stress and anxiety comes from your focus on what you fear might happen, as opposed to what's actually happening. Stress comes when your mind goes off into the land of negative "what ifs," and your imagination runs wild in the direction of your fears. But more often than not, these fears are complete fabrications based only on your insecurities and nothing more.

What you think, feel, believe, and do is your choice. You can choose to fear the future, you can choose to regret the past, or you can choose to believe in love, joy, and peace, and fill your present moments accordingly. Instead of thinking of the worst case scenario, you can choose to think about and expect the best. You can change your "what ifs" into positive expectations at any time because it is within your power to do so.

Positive thinking gets you focused on and naturally visualizing positive outcomes, and this then enlivens you with positive feelings. But keep in mind that while positive thinking can be very powerful, it is not a substitute for dealing with your core beliefs. If you just think positive thoughts without dealing with your true feelings, which may be doubtful and negative, your repressed feelings will be your point of attraction.

So, to ensure that your positive thoughts do indeed show up in your life as positive expressions, you need to be honest with yourself about how you truly feel and what you truly believe. This type of introspection will transform vacant words, thoughts, and actions into powerful fuel for the manifestation of what you truly love.

Releasing fear and anxiety is a lot easier to do when you are able to get present and affirm your truth. Conversely, when you allow your mind to wander off to unpleasant places, you end up creating an illusionary world where you have no control over your emotions or reactions. What you think about feels very real to you, even though it often has no merit at all. Anxiety is regularly caused by these wandering thoughts of negativity, as well as the repressed emotions that ensue, so stop these thoughts in their tracks. Ground yourself in the present moment and affirm your truth. This will automatically release the illusions that have been causing you so much stress and struggle in your life.

The beautiful thing about being present is realizing that each moment brings you a choice. You can choose to fill the new moment up with old negative patterns. Or you can choose to create something better and more freeing. This moment right now is like no other. It is unique and new. So use this opportunity to break the cycle of fear and anxiety for good. Stop projecting your past into your future and start appreciating the present as the gift that it is.

Understand that fear comes from build-up. It comes when you build up negative expectations and then project them into your future. However, when you are aware of the present moment, those negative and fearful hypothetical scenarios simply dissolve on their own. This is because you are no longer feeding them with your focus. Focus on this moment right now. Don't worry about what may come. Just deal with one moment at a time while having positive expectations for your future.

If you are not happy with what you are feeling or experiencing right now, know that it's only because you're not bothering to change your thoughts, feelings, beliefs, and/or actions. You cannot change anything without changing something. Meaning, you cannot create different results by continuing with the same patterns over and over. All it really takes is a change in consciousness. It may feel uncomfortable at first but it's well worth the investment. Once you change your focus from fear to certainty and from worry to trust, you will be well on your way to making positive changes in your life, and you will attract the circumstances and knowledge necessary to do so.

We waste so much energy worrying about the future, worrying about things we cannot change, worrying about things we want to change but we feel we can't, or worrying about the "mistakes" we've made in our lives. But this is very illogical. We worry as if we think it will help our situation in some way, but worry only makes things worse. We do not prevent what we worry about by worrying about it, so we might as well stop worrying about it, right? Act on what you can control and let go of what you can't. Be present and accepting of where you are and trust that it's all being taken care of in the best of ways.

We also spend an excessive amount of energy worrying about hypothetical situations that involve what we don't want. If we could only spend as much energy thinking about, expecting, and feeling the truth of what we do want as if we already have it, we could greatly alter our point of attraction to actually receive what we need and love the most. If we could simply enjoy the moment for its own sake we could alter our vibration to such a positive degree that the essence of what we love would freely manifest into our lives. It's simply a matter of choice. All we need to do is shift our focus onto what authentically feels good, and subsequently, we'll attract more of what authentically feels good into our lives.

When you take control of your focus and you bring it into the present, your fears and anxiety suddenly dissipate. You become grounded in the truth, and with truth there can be no fear. Know that you can handle what's put in front of you. Have faith that you are taken care of. Let go to something bigger than yourself; to the Energy Source from which you emanate and with which you are one. When faced with fear, get grounded in the present moment and focus on the good. This will give you perspective on where you may be giving your power away to illusions.

Trust that just because you are experiencing something you don't like in the moment, that doesn't mean it will necessarily be permanent. Fear will have you thinking, "This is it," but the truth is that it's not. We are dynamic and we are renewed in every moment. There is always an opportunity for positive change. Just get grounded in the truth, and in your alignment with it, and realize that at your core you are true well-being in all aspects of your life, right now, and always.

If you want to change something you can, but you can't do it by thinking the same thoughts, feeling the same feelings, and doing the same things in the same ways. You do it by changing the cause so that you change the effect. You do it by embracing the essence of who you want to be, and realizing that this essence is who you are already.

Know that giving into your fears, doubts, regrets, and insecurities will never get you to where you want to be; it will only perpetuate the state from which you want to escape. Learn to trust and let go. Learn to have faith. Realize the truth of who you really are, and then all your fear, doubt, regret, insecurity, and stress will simply cease to exist.

Stress:

We often hear about the need for stress-reduction and managing stress, but is it possible to eliminate stress altogether? What is stress anyway?

Stress is your response to something external to you that has caused a reaction within you. While stress can come from within, in actuality, it is caused by your interpretations of yourself in relation to your outside world. Your internal thoughts and feelings, then, are simply responding consciously or subconsciously to something you perceive from outside of you that you are now internalizing as a part of you. You notice, you filter, you absorb, and you internalize.

Used as a verb, however, stress can be defined as placing emphasis onto something. In this case, you can use stress to your advantage in that you can choose the focus of your liking, and then put your emphasis on that focus. That means you can choose the perceptions that are positive and up-lifting to you rather than those that are destructive and depressing.

Understand that it's not so much about eliminating stress as it is about transforming it into something more positive. It's about seeing stress as a motivator rather than something that limits you. The key lies in changing your perceptions so that you can transform your stress into feelings of excitement and enthusiasm instead.

Stress is often caused by our anticipation of future events, regretful thoughts of the past, or our inability to see our present moments as peaceful and opportune. It's created when we get lost in the chase for happiness so much so that we fail to see the blessings we already have in our lives right now. This lack of appreciation and presence, then, creates a stressful environment where all we see are obstacles and road blocks.

Stress comes from fear. However, if we transform our fear, our stress will go with it. It is through understanding our fears that we are able to uproot them. And when we uproot them, our stress turns into enthusiasm because we know that we no longer have anything standing in our way. It's from understanding our perceptions too that we are able to transform what we perceive as stressful or fearful situations into opportunities and learning experiences.

The way stress affects you is a matter of how you choose to define it. It's how you use it and how you perceive it that matters most. So don't see it as something that causes you hardship. See it instead as something that invigorates you. In fact, change the definition of it altogether and choose to see it as excitement, enthusiasm, and motivation. By interpreting stress in a positive way you will actually be able to eliminate it because you will no longer see it as something that's necessarily negative.

We all feel stressed at one time or another. Let's face it, the unknown freaks us out sometimes. And because we are often faced with the unknown we tend to allow ourselves to feel stressed-out. So the key then is to simply let go and have faith. Enjoy the moment at hand and do your best with what you have. Change how you see your external conditions so that you can move out of stress and into peace and productivity. Know that you can think and feel your way out of stress simply by changing your perceptions and subsequent actions and reactions.

So as you move forward in your life, every time you feel stress building within you, get present and realize the true cause of it. Because the more present you are in your awareness, the more you will realize the nature of your stress, and the more you will be able to transform it.

APPLICATION:

Fear is one of the biggest factors, if not the biggest factor involved in sabotaging one's ability to live a fulfilling life. Once you learn to release your fears, however, you will become unlimited in what you can be, do, and have.

Releasing Fear:

To start releasing your fears, ask yourself this: what are you truly afraid of? Does your fear really have any merit or is it something you've fabricated in your mind? Question your negative assumptions. What negative perceptions and/or beliefs have you taken on in the creation of your life?

The cool thing is that when you get into questioning your fears, your fears suddenly come into perspective and lose steam. So question the validity of your fears and then shift your focus onto the opposite of what you fear might happen. For instance, instead of thinking in terms of what you're afraid of, think in terms of what you love and what authentically feels good to you. What do you want to experience right now?

Then think about this: what would you do right now if you had no fears or worries? How would you feel? Can you imagine it, a life full of peace, joy, security, and utter fulfillment? Dwell in this reality for a while and feel it in your heart. If you find yourself in the midst of a fearful thought, just stop and ask yourself, "Where am I right now and what's really going on?" This will immediately bring you back into the present moment where you can actively choose to align with the truth that you are one with wellness now and always.

With that said, while it's easy to affirm your wellness when you feel well, it can be quite challenging to do when you don't. At these times it's easy to allow fear to take over. But do not be fooled by outward appearances. Know that you have allowed these circumstances to materialize in your life through your misaligned thinking, but that you can also allow your natural well-being to emerge by altering that thinking. It's simply a matter of taking responsibility. It is not a game of self-blame. Rather, it's an understanding that you are not a victim and that you have the power within you to change your circumstances for the better if you so choose.

At your core you are truly well. You simply need to align with that reality, that feeling, and that truth in your consciousness, and sooner than you think your external circumstances will rise up to match that which you already know is true.

So, instead of allowing your mind to wander to unpleasant places, think of what you do want, what you do like, and think of the possibility of that possibility. This will bring your attention onto something that feels good rather than something that does not.

Understand that fear often comes when we obsess about hypothetical situations that don't feel good. This then causes anxiety and stress to build up within us. To deal with this anxiety, stress, and fear simply follow these steps below to help ground you in the present moment, and in the truth that you are just fine as you are:

1. Accept your feelings. Don't fight against them, deny them, or even want them to go away. All this does is create more resistance within you, which ends up perpetuating the anxiety you are feeling. Instead, welcome your feelings. Let them be. Notice them without judging them. Notice the sensations within your body as objectively as you can. Instead of fighting how you feel, let it flow through and out of you. This may seem hard to do at first, because your body's natural response is fight or flight, but the more you stop giving your fears power through your resistance and focus on them, the faster they will naturally dissipate.

2. Next, ask yourself if the threat you perceive is real or imagined? Is it a reality right now or something you fear for the future? If there is no apparent threat in the moment, realize that there is nothing to fear right now. Take your attention off of what you fear and place it onto what you love, what you appreciate, what you desire to experience, and then feel that as your truth and reality right now. Your thoughts

are your own, so just like you can choose fearful ones, you can choose peaceful ones too.

3. Engage your senses. What are you experiencing right now? Notice what's around you. Do your best to notice positive things, things that feel good, things that you can appreciate right now. It can be as simple as feeling the sun on your face or taking a sip of a comforting cup of tea. Noticing your experiences in the moment is not about dwelling on things that don't feel good, but rather appreciating those things that do. This will ground you in the experience of the moment, shift your perceptions, and get you away from thinking about all those hypothetical scenarios that are driving you crazy with worry.

4. If you are going to think in terms of "what ifs," be sure to think only in terms of the positive feelings you anticipate, like, for example, "What if all goes well?" "What if I'm just fine?" "What if I find that activity to be enjoyable?" "What if I could be totally confident?" "What if I overcame my fears?" and so on. Know that you drive your consciousness, and that you can choose the direction in which it goes. You have this power within you. Transform your nervous anticipation into excitement. This way you expect, intend, and attract what you love and enjoy instead of what you fear. Change your perceptions and you will change not only your feelings, but also your results. Then, as you shift your perceptions, take action in spite of your fears because 1) you know it's an irrational fear anyway, and 2) facing your fears will give you the confidence to continue to move forward.

5. Finally, to help ensure that your anxiety does not resurface, examine the possible sources of your anxiety. What's truly going on within you that's causing your fear, stress, and anxiety to manifest right now? Getting to the root of your anxiety proactively and objectively can help you eliminate it for good. But it's much easier to get to the root and release the main cause of your stress, fear, and anxiety when you are present and grounded in the moment, rather than caught up

in panic, so go through the above steps first to get you grounded and thinking proactively.

Releasing Guilt and Regret:

Regret and guilt are very unhealthy emotions. They keep you stuck in the past and unable to move forward, which causes you to attract the same negative patterns over and over again. But at some point you need to learn what you can learn, do what you can do, and then move on.

The first step in releasing guilt and regret is to understand that what's done is done. You may not be able to physically change the past, but you can certainly let it go and resolve to do things differently from now on. You can learn from it and then change your perception of it, your reaction to it, your feelings about it, and subsequently, the effect it has on your life from this point on.

It's one thing to be introspective and think about a better way for you to handle yourself in the future, just don't get too caught up in wondering, "What if I had done things differently?" Know that even if your behavior or action was different, it may not have necessarily changed the ultimate outcome of things anyway. Other people and their free will were involved too, so no matter what you could have done differently, it doesn't guarantee that the outcome would have been any different. And maybe it needed to be that way.

It's extremely important to note that while it's good to take responsibility for your own actions, it is counter-productive to take on the responsibilities of others. Meaning, do not take ownership of someone else's actions by excusing their behavior while belittling your own. And do not be manipulated into apologizing for something you didn't do. Regret is a funny emotion because sometimes it comes from our own self-loathing and guilt. Releasing regret, then, can symbolize your respect for yourself and your willingness to hold others accountable for their own actions. Everyone plays a role in every interaction. Figure out your part in it, but allow others the chance to learn from theirs as well.

Also, understand that releasing regret is not about denying what happened. Rather, it's about transforming your feelings about what happened so that you can move forward with more proactive behavior. If you're constantly replaying a regret in your mind, if you are wallowing in guilt and are unable to forgive yourself, this will not only negatively impact your own life, it will also prevent you from sharing what you have to share with others.

Regret is a negative emotion and a complete misalignment from who you truly are. Of course it's natural to feel remorseful for your negative behavior. But it's not productive to allow that feeling to take over your entire life. Think of it this way, if someone you knew came to you with apology, taking responsibility for their actions, showing you their true remorse, vowing they would do better, and then actually doing better, would you be able to forgive them? If so, couldn't you afford yourself that same generosity? If not, why not? Do you not deserve a second chance too? Know that you are in a learning process, just like everybody else, and that sometimes you might blunder. But know too that the truth of your character will be revealed by what you do next. However, you must in fact go forward and do better; otherwise you'll be a prisoner of those same negative patterns that have been holding you back up until this point.

If you are regretful about a decision or a "mistake" you think you made, know that there was a reason for it. Sometimes it pays to know what you don't want so that you can be clearer about what you do want. Sometimes it pays to know what not to do so that you know what to do. And sometimes it's better not to label something as a "mistake" until all the pieces of the puzzle have come together, because sometimes what you think is a mistake is in fact no mistake at all. In fact, it can be the step that takes you to where you want to be, even if it does come cloaked in mystery or appearances you don't yet understand. Sometimes the way to let go is to make the mistake, learn from it, and come out the other end with a new perspective.

Most of all, realize that as we learn and grow into our full potential we may make some blunders along the way. The key, however, is to realize that life is a learning process. So give yourself some leeway. Just like you wouldn't scold a baby for falling down while learning to walk, you needn't be so hard on yourself either. Be gentle with yourself. Trust in your ability to learn and grow, and then use that ability to choose thoughts and actions that support you in being your best self.

Realize that this moment is new and fresh and available for you to mold into anything you want, regardless of what happened before. Know that you can release old patterns from your past and embrace the freshness of the present moment. So don't use your past to determine your future. Start creating the life you want to live right now.

Declare, "I am whole, I am complete, I am well-being, now and always." Feel this as your truth. Know that the Life Force flowing through you has the power to create, restore, and maintain all your wealth, health, joy, and all your well-being in an instant, if you simply realize that this perfection is what and who you are at your core. Believe it, feel it, and be it now.

Life is meant to be enjoyed and experienced to its fullest. Don't let fear or regret stop you from this joy. Trust The Universe. Trust the Life Force moving through you. Release your worries and stop imposing your fears onto yourself and onto others. Expect the best for all. Have positive expectations for your future while living patiently, joyously, and presently in each moment.

Health, peace, love, trust, purpose, freedom, wealth, and overall total well-being…focus on these essences and your fears, worries, and regrets will naturally dissipate. Trust in the process of life. Relax with peace of mind knowing that Divine Intelligence has everything under perfect control.

Getting Closure:

When we feel a lack of closure or we feel rejected by a person or situation, the ego can sometimes get carried away with over-analysis. It can drive us crazy as we obsess over it and play it back in our minds trying to figure out why it happened, and perhaps even what we could have done differently. Ego makes us desire retribution and validation, and as a result, it makes us lose our sense for what we actually want and what's actually important.

But why dwell on something that's essentially out of your hands? Why not choose to move on to something better and more positive, something that feels good? It doesn't make logical sense to dwell on the past, but then again, the ego defies logic sometimes.

Don't look for retribution; it will only waste your time, and it's unlikely that it will end the way you want it to anyway. You may get the last word but it just won't be worth it. To gratify your ego and have that be your sole motivator will only take you farther away from your purpose and true fulfillment. It's self-sabotaging so don't do it.

Look past your ego's desire and see what it is you really want. Do you really want that position at work that passed you by, or were you just hoping it would make you feel better about yourself or perhaps make others see you in a better light? Do you really want to be with that guy or girl who rejected you, or do you just want the control because your ego was bruised? And even if you really did want it (the job, the relationship), it obviously doesn't want you at this time, so instead of dwelling on it, move past it so that you can attract what is right for you; because what's right for you wants you too. Think about it, is it more important to get retribution and ego validation, or is it more important to move on with your life and start focusing on and manifesting something better? Don't let your ego get carried away, because if you do, you will only be hurting your own progress towards a better life.

Stop making the same mistakes over and over again. That's what this experience of yours is likely trying to show you. Instead of falling into your same ego patterns, listen and learn, and then just move on. You'll be better off for it. Don't question your own worth. Just look for the feedback and move on with better action that's more aligned with who you really are and what you really want. Let go of your need for closure and you will get it that much sooner.

When a relationship or job, or whatever the case may be, has come to an unexplained and/or abrupt end, yes, it can sometimes seem difficult to move on without getting the proper closure for it. It's human nature to want to understand, but sometimes it may take a while, or maybe you'll never truly know. So if you need closure and you're not getting it from someone else, create it for yourself.

Do it through having faith and trust in the bigger picture. Do it through your detachment from the outcome. While you can assess what happened and learn from it, there comes a point when you just have to let go. You can hypothesize all you want, and you may even be on the money with your theories, but unless you know the exact perspective of the other side, you may still have unanswered questions.

So to get closure simply let go of your need to know. Understand yourself and your role in it, but let go of the rest. Learn from it and then move on. Trust that you'll know what you need to know on a need-to-know basis. While it can be comforting to think about and analyze the other person's perspective for the sake of your own understanding, don't waste too much time trying to figure out what another person was thinking, or why they did what they did. Focus on what it's showing you in your life and what you can do about it from your end.

Forgive yourself and forgive the other parties involved too. This doesn't mean you have to agree with their choices or decisions, or even tolerate their behavior. Simply know that there are reasons behind what happened, and that while there are lessons in it for you too, sometimes those reasons really have nothing to do with you. Perhaps the company you worked for needed to downsize? Perhaps your romantic interest had his/her own insecurities to deal with? Yes, you attracted those circumstances into your life, and that's cause for introspection, but that doesn't mean you need to take everything personally either. So let it go without feeling resentful. Trust that it's all for the best and instead of dwelling on what might have been, learn the lesson and then focus on taking the next steps towards something you love. Know that if something or someone is right for you, it/they will want you in return.

Don't obsess about what happened or rehash it in your mind over and over again. Just let go and trust. Closure comes from your ability to accept the moment as it is, and accept that other people may not approve of you, or even like you. Closure comes from being ok with that, and then just focusing on being your best self, and knowing that this is always good enough.

So what if you're being judged? So what if someone's impression of you is not accurate by your own standards? Why do you need their approval anyway? Know that your self-esteem and self-worth need not depend on anyone else but you. You have to be good with yourself and love yourself no matter what others think of you. You have to be able to let go of your need for approval and feel free to just be your true self.

At the end of the day, closure comes from your decision to close the door on something. But know that once you do, another door will open for you. So stop lingering on the closed door and start looking for other openings. Stop chasing after closure and just create it for yourself. Then once you've let go of your need for closure, that's when you'll finally get it.

One great technique for helping you get closure is to write in a journal. It's a fantastic way to express your thoughts and feelings and to help you get to the core cause and subsequent resolution for your issue. So start writing. Keep writing until you feel you've gotten everything out. What this does is not only help you vent; it also helps bring new perspective to the situation. Let all your anger, hurt, resentment, frustration, self-pity, and confusion leave you. Think about the lessons and the positive side of things instead, and simply be optimistic for the future. Be in the moment by choosing to trust the process that is your life's path.

Once you are done, if a resolution is not yet clear, just let it go. After journaling you will likely feel better and clearer about things anyway, as well as less reactive. Journaling can also help you avoid taking impulsive action, because after you've finished exploring your feelings and motives you'll have a better perspective on whether or not what you wanted to do earlier is actually the best option. When you let out steam in this proactive way you actually end up creating your own closure, and as a result, you become more level-headed with your choices and more capable of moving on.

Another technique for getting closure is to simply write a letter addressed to the person in question. You don't have to send it, just use it as an outlet to express your feelings in an open and honest way. This will help you feel like you've been heard, even if the person never receives it. It will help you clear the energy and your focus so that you can finally move on to better thoughts. It can help you get to a place of peace, acceptance, clarity, and closure, all on your own.

Know that proactively expressing yourself to others is important, as it can be beneficial for you and for them. But if the opportunity hasn't presented itself, for your own sake, a letter like this can bring you the closure and perspective you need in the moment to move on.

Releasing Stress:

Remember, stress is based a lot on your perceptions. How you perceive the events in your life, and how you respond to them, has a lot to do with the level of stress you will feel, and subsequently, how these events will play out in your life. If you let yourself feel overly stressed this can have an adverse effect on all areas of your life. For this reason, it's important to be mindful of where you are feeling stressed and why, and then take action to transform it.

So make a list right now of the situations in your life that you find stressful. Then go down the list, one by one, and think of how you can change your perception of each situation.

For example, say your commute to work is stressing you out. Instead of thinking about all the traffic, the time it takes you, the angry people on the road, and so on, think about what you can do with this time that will be more productive. For instance, you could choose to put on some calming music and use this time to relax before your workday begins. You could choose to think about all those things you appreciate about your life, starting with the fact that you have a job to go to in the first place. You could choose whatever feels good to you. After all, the traffic isn't going to change just because you're stressed out about it, so you might as well ride the wave, and enjoy the ride while you're at it. Before you know it, you will have arrived at work in less time than you thought and without being all stressed-out.

Releasing Hidden Anxiety:

Sometimes our fears and worries manifest themselves in ways we don't completely understand or maybe even recognize. And if we are not present and aware we'll likely miss the connection between events, as well as the subconscious thoughts that are creating anxiety in our lives from within.

Sometimes our anxiety appears to come from "out of the blue." And even further, it can manifest itself as random physical symptoms we can't seem to explain, or as patterns in our lives that seem to leave us dumbfounded. While it's important not to ignore physical symptoms, or patterns, it's just as important to recognize the metaphysical causes for them, because everything starts in consciousness before it manifests in form or experience.

Sometimes we feel anxious but don't even know it because it manifests itself in seemingly unrelated ways. Maybe it's manifesting itself as anger, sadness, frustration, or something else. But "out of the blue" experiences are really triggered by something deeper. In order to figure out what those triggers are you need to start asking yourself some questions. Be honest with your answers, though, because repressing how you truly feel or what you truly want will only end up hurting you in the end.

Stress is nothing to laugh at. It causes more disharmony in your system and in your life than you might think. But stress can be very revealing too, if you know where to look. If you are feeling stressed, burned out, unappreciated, depressed, or the like, it's time to ask yourself, "What exactly is going on here?" "What are my emotions, my life, my body, my experiences trying to tell me?" If you don't bother asking these questions you will likely repress your true feelings, which will only cause more of these circumstances to occur.

So sit down, get quiet, and ask yourself about how you truly feel. Start by noticing how stress manifests itself within your body. Notice any patterns of thought, feeling, or external circumstances that keep occurring in your life. Think about each area of your life, like your work, your relationships, your family, your finances, your health, your body, your self-image, etc. and assess what feelings come up for each one. This exercise is not one to rush through and it could take a few times of doing before you are clear on what's truly going on. But the more you delve into your subconscious mind, and the more present and aware you become of your body, your thoughts, your feelings, and the circumstances in your life, the more you'll get to the root of your anxiety, which will help you release it for good.

Affirmations:

Affirmations can certainly be helpful in re-programming your subconscious mind, and often that's what's needed to release certain fears and negative patterns from your life. However, it's important to note that affirmations are most effective when you do not hold resistance to them.

If you use positive affirmations to counter your fears and insecurities, you'll need to ensure that you are not just masking your true feelings with idealized words. You cannot hide from your true feelings. In fact, the more you try to cover them up, the more resistance you will create within yourself.

You can certainly repeat positive affirmations over and over again with the hope of convincing yourself of something, and eventually this might work. But it's much more effective to find something you can believe as your truth now and affirm that with proactive gratitude.

Understand that if you do not deal with your true emotions and faulty beliefs now, you can affirm what you want over and over until you're blue in the face, and maybe even get it, but it may not be long before your old patterns and old fears start to resurface again. Why? Because if there is a contradiction between your conscious intentions, your present reality, and your subconscious beliefs, this can create resistance within you that can then cause delay or stagnation in your manifestation process.

While you can re-program your subconscious mind with repeated mantras, it may be easier to start with mantras that are at least somewhat believable to you. Understand that it's unlikely that you will spend every moment of every day repeating one affirmation after another. As such, it's important that when you are busy with other things, and consequently not affirming what you want at that time, that you are still choosing thoughts, feelings, and actions that back your affirmations. If you affirm something but then go right back into old negative patterns again, your affirmations won't mean much at all. So pick something that you can consistently keep up throughout your day because you know that it's ultimately true.

For instance, you can tell yourself you are wealthy, but if you continue to take actions that contradict that statement, those actions will be reflecting your true beliefs, and your affirmation won't mean much at all. People often wonder why their affirmations don't take hold, and the one major reason is because they are saying something over and over without really feeling it as a possibility or a reality, and as a result, their actions don't match and they end up getting something totally contradictory to what they actually want.

So instead of affirming something you don't feel is true, first ask yourself why you don't believe in it. Figure out what negative belief is preventing you from manifesting what you love. Then pose another question like, "What if what I desire is possible for me?" This will in turn move you away from resistance and towards belief.

Save yourself the time and effort. Affirm what you can actually believe now rather than trying to convince yourself of something you're not sure is true. Or at the very least, believe in its possibility. You don't have to take giant leaps right away. You can start smaller and then grow your belief from there. Understand that the less resistance you have to what you are saying in the moment, the faster your affirmations will take hold, and the more likely you will see your affirmations manifesting in your life. Know that you can certainly change a habit or life circumstance by repeating an affirmation over and over, but you'll speed up the process considerably by releasing your resistance to what you are affirming first.

For instance, saying, "I am a billionaire" when you feel it's not currently true causes a contradiction between what you're saying and what you are actually feeling and believing. So instead say, "I am wealthy in mind, body, and spirit," or "I am growing richer and richer by the moment." These are just examples, but they show you how to re-word your affirmations so that they re-program your beliefs without creating resistance within you.

In addition to affirming what you believe, focus on the essence of what you want to attract into your life; things like health, love, prosperity, joy, security, and so on. Embrace these essences as your truth right now, and then pay attention to the energy behind your words, because it is the energy that draws to you and not your words alone.

When you focus your affirmations on the feeling, essence, and/or behavioral pattern that you want to achieve, i.e. the things that you can control (like your perception), there is less likelihood that resistance will build up within you. For example, if you want to be fearless then repeating, "I am fearless" over and over can help you eventually feel fearless as you re-program your subconscious mind into believing that this is true. Then, as you act on this affirmation (i.e. act with confidence and peace of mind) you will be strengthening that belief, which will help it take hold even faster.

However, if while you are telling yourself that you are fearless you keep acting on your fears and allowing them to control you, it can take longer for your affirmation to take hold. In this case, it would be wise to understand and face your fears rather than running away from them or sweeping them under the rug. To help you find the courage to face your fears you can then affirm something like, "I am capable of being fearless," or "I am capable of letting go of my fears," or even, "What if I were fearless?" Then take action steps that match those statements, one step and one moment at a time.

Now, if you state a concrete affirmation like the achievement of a goal that has yet to happen, it may cause resistance within you if you don't really believe that it's real or that it's possible for you to manifest. For instance, if you say, "I am a successful business owner," but that's not your current physical reality, and you're feeling fearful and insecure because of that, the more you say it, the more resistance it can cause within you. In this case, focusing on an essence may be more beneficial.

So you can state, "I am successful,' or even just, "I am success." This way you are stating an essence that can mean an infinite amount of things. You can then feel this essence right now as your truth and pick out ways that this essence already exists in your life, like through another project or task you've completed, a memory of a successful time in your life, or even an awareness of the success of those around you.

You can also choose to rephrase your affirmations to state something you can actually believe right now, something like, "Every day I am becoming more and more successful," or "Every day I am expressing my inherent success more and more." These statements do not challenge your current state of belief so they can lead you to your manifestations that much faster by preventing unnecessary delay caused by resistance.

So while affirmations can be very effective in re-programming your subconscious mind to release fearful, regretful, and overall negative beliefs, thoughts, and feelings, choose a manner that will create the least resistance within you. Create affirmations that will actually help you shape the physical reality you desire to experience rather than just being empty words that cause more frustration and stagnation in your life.

Remember, any practice in which you partake needs to be one that benefits you rather than contradicts what you want to achieve. So in this case, in order to get the most out of your affirmations start by being present and aware, because by being present and aware you will quickly recognize any contradictions and any resistance you are creating within yourself.

Affirmations can certainly help you re-program your subconscious beliefs, however, when you start with present awareness first, you shorten your learning curve because you become aware of your true feelings. And when you are aware of your true feelings, you don't end up wasting years of your life affirming something only to realize that you've been contradicting yourself the whole time from within.

You are the only one who truly knows what works for you. If your affirmations are taking hold and manifesting in your life in a positive way, then great, keep doing what you're doing. But, if you have been affirming something for a while and not seeing anything change, perhaps this is your cue to get present and start noticing where you are resisting your good from coming to you. Ask yourself questions like, "What do I want?" "Why do I want it?" "How will it feel when I get it?" "How do I feel about my ability to have it?" and most importantly, "Where is my focus right now? Is it on what I love and enjoy, or am I complaining about what I dislike, what I feel I can't have, or what I believe isn't possible for me?"

Visualize what you love, affirm it, and be conscious enough in the present moment to see what comes up. Do you feel any resistance in your body? Are you feeling anxious, impatient, or are you feeling enthusiastic and hopeful? Do you really believe that what you are affirming is possible for you?

Make it a practice in your life to recognize what you want to be, do, and have. Then ask yourself how you feel about your ability to be, do, and have it. Clear any resistance within you. Choose affirmations that presently state what you already know is true for you; something you can feel in the moment without contradiction. Then affirm this truth with confidence.

Realize that it's really about efficiency. Rather than just repeating your way into new beliefs by bombarding your mind with affirmations and intentions, notice how you are feeling about what you are saying to yourself. If you want to get to your results of feeling good faster and more consistently, deal with your resistance first by being present enough to recognize if it's there. And if it is there, do something about it.

Meditation:

Sit in a comfortable position keeping your hands open and palms facing up. Take a few deep breaths at your own pace. As you do, envision a loving and powerful energy moving through you with every inhaled breath. Imagine all of your negative beliefs, negative thoughts, and negative feelings, along with your worries, fears, doubts, insecurities, and regrets being released from you with every exhaled breath.

Feel the Life Force moving through you, lovingly filling your awareness with truth, love, and joy. Feel your personal energy growing brighter and brighter from your core, like a bright light, filling your entire body, filling the space around you, and then emanating out into the world and beyond. Now sit with this feeling for a moment.

Now, instead of focusing on what you fear or regret, focus on what you want to feel. Focus on the essence you want to express, such as peace of mind, trust, love, joy, and anything else you value. Visualize that you are in a place that feels safe, with people you love. Feel your heart fill up with appreciation and joy. Give yourself permission to feel free, to feel at peace. Take your time with this. Sit with this feeling for as long as it feels appropriate to you.

When you're ready, slowly bring your attention back to your physical body. Ground yourself by feeling the earth, ground, floor, or seat beneath you, and by bringing your attention back to your surroundings.

Now get up and go about your day knowing that the essence of what you desire is already yours, within you, and manifesting in the perfect time and order. Know that you are whole and complete right now, and act from this place of confidence and trust in every moment.

Align your thoughts, feelings, beliefs, and actions with your authentic desires and intentions rather than with your fears and regrets. Make sure that your consciousness is positive and patient. Have faith, have trust, and go about your daily activities with a positive attitude. Any time a fear arises within you, go back to the exercises you've learned here and eventually you will free yourself from feelings of uncertainty, and you will embrace the truth; that all is truly well, right now, and always.

Chapter 13:
Appreciation

A simple "thank you" is enough to change your entire life for the better.

At any given moment you are either appreciating something or you are depreciating it. Which one you choose to do is up to you. It may sound like a cliché but life is in fact about perception; whether you see the glass as half empty, half full, or overflowing. When you choose to perceive your life as full and complete, however, this is when you are most empowered. When you choose to focus on all that you have to be grateful for, this is when you attract more joy into your life.

Half full or half empty is simply an interpretation, a perception. So be full in the sense that you know you have it in you to be happy right now. But be empty in the sense of knowing that you are a vessel ready to be filled and fulfilled by all of your potential. Strip yourself of worry and doubt and continue to explore and expand your reality to fit with the truth you already know exists within you. Know that you are a channel, a beautiful vehicle through which Source Energy flows and overflows into every area of your life. Know that you always have more than enough to share with others too.

Appreciation is about understanding that your life is truly a blessing. Sure, you can look at the circumstances in your life that you don't particularly like and use those as justifications for not appreciating, but that will only give you more to complain about. Understand that when you dwell on your regrets of the past, or fear for your future, you are not appreciating. When you are thinking in terms of lack, you are not appreciating. When you are jealous of what others have, you are not appreciating. When you are feeling sorry for yourself, you are not appreciating. And as a result of all this negative focus, you are only creating more chaos in your life.

But you can always find something to appreciate. You can always choose to focus on the abundance in your life right now, because it is there, even in the smallest of ways. If you really pay attention you are guaranteed to find something you can appreciate right now. The point is to choose to see the best in everything because your perceptions will determine what you attract into your life, plain and simple.

If you understand how energy circulates you also understand that when you appreciate, you attract more of which to appreciate. Be appreciative for its own sake. Be genuine in how you feel. Don't just look for the rewards it will bring you. Feel it as an honest expression of gratitude. Appreciate as your way of being in every moment rather than just as a means to another end.

You cannot fake appreciation. It's not just about the words you speak or even the actions you take. It's about how you truly feel inside. When you sincerely appreciate something, you feel it in your heart. It is never something you have to force. It is simply something you need to awaken within yourself.

Be proactive in your appreciation. Focus less on relief and more on joy, because when you are proactively grateful, you don't need any wake-up calls to stimulate your gratitude. Let appreciation be your way of life rather than just another exercise you force upon yourself from time to time. This way your gratitude will always be authentic. Appreciate as your way of being; just because. Sure, appreciate what you have, but also appreciate simply who you are and where you come from, i.e. the Energy Source that is infinite and all-loving.

Appreciate from a place of fullness. Appreciate from a place of inner bliss. Be in a place where you never need to compare or measure, and where you feel grateful for all the blessings in your life naturally and honestly.

Expressing genuine gratitude is a great way of sharing with others too. So go ahead, tell people what you appreciate about them. Express thanks to all those around you for whom you feel grateful. Don't expect that people owe you something, and don't take anything or anyone for granted.

Appreciation

Appreciation is truly one of the most powerful tools you can use to generate authentic happiness and success in your life. It sounds like a simple concept, and we hear about it all the time, but it's not something to be underestimated. Learn to appreciate as your way of life, and good things will naturally flow to you, and through you, with ease and joy.

APPLICATION:

Think of something or even someone you've been taking for granted lately. Make it a point to appreciate it/them right now in this very moment. Let the appreciation fill your heart and every part of you. Now go out and express this gratitude. Perform random acts of kindness and start a domino effect that will change the course of so many people's lives for the better. Use positive and appreciative language when speaking to others and to yourself. Be an up-lifter.

The more you feel appreciative about life, the more of a positive impact you will have on others, and the more you will magnetize to yourself more for which to be grateful. Be thankful for the gifts others bestow upon you and for all that you have to share with them too. Give The Universe a clear signal that you are open to receiving its bounty, which is indeed your birthright. Say a simple "thank you" every day for the joys in your life, and even for the lessons, and you will experience what you came here for, i.e. true joy, genuine love, and total fulfillment.

You can even make a daily gratitude list. Do this each night before bed and you will set a positive tone for each day to follow. As you list what you appreciate, truly feel it in the present moment. Get into the feelings of proactive gratitude right now and let this be your new habit of awareness on a daily basis. But don't stop at appreciating things that are external to you. Appreciate life itself. Appreciate your inner peace and power too.

Know that when you complain about your life, or the people in your life, you are taking yourself away from appreciating. By doing so you not only devalue what you have, you also place yourself on a vibration that attracts more frustration into your life. Appreciation is not just something to do when things are going well. It's an exercise to partake in at all times, perhaps especially when things aren't going well. Because if things aren't going the way you'd like them to, it's likely because somewhere along the way you weren't appreciating as much as you could have been.

Appreciation

Release your agendas with people, release your attachments to outcomes, and instead, embrace the moment for what you make of it, for the opportunity that it presents to appreciate life for its own sake. Appreciate the differences between people, even if you don't agree with them. And although it's hard to do, appreciate those moments where you feel frustrated, because those moments are teaching you something important. And if you accept the lesson, you will get that much closer to living the life you ultimately love.

The more you get into the habit of being present and appreciating everything as a blessing, as a lesson, as guidance, or however you choose to positively perceive it in the moment, the more you will create a strong momentum that will place you on the path of your purpose and total joy. As long as what you perceive is positive and uplifting, you will be well on your way to a daily life of true happiness, peace, and success.

Chapter 14:
Detachment from the Outcome

What's yours is yours. You needn't rush it and you needn't chase after it. If it's right, it's right.

Without realizing it we have become a very needy bunch, dependent on things external to us to make us happy. We live in a very consumerist society that values materialism and getting ahead over all else. Mind you, the physical aspects of life, including material wealth and tangible success, are not things to be shunned. It's just that we have become so obsessed with the achievement of them that we've failed to notice anything else. Subsequently, in our attempts to get what we think will make us happy, we've ended up more depressed and more frustrated than ever before. But what's at the root of all this?

We are very goal-oriented. We set timelines and micro-manage details. As such, we have created an environment for ourselves of great pressure and stress. We have become so attached to the outcome of things that we've ignored what's real and true.

Living in a present state of awareness, however, brings us back to what is authentic and pure. It gives us the chance to look at our lives and our values and determine what's most important to us. It gives us the opportunity to listen to our true calling, a task that's impossible to do when we are stuck in tunnel-vision.

When we are attached to an outcome it puts us in a very compromising and desperate position. It prompts us to manipulate the people and circumstances around us so that we get our way, but in doing so we end up closing ourselves off from true inspiration, intuition, guidance, and flow.

To avoid being cut off from flow you must never be so attached to one outcome that you lose perspective on the opportunities that are right in front of you. You must lose your need for approval and fear of rejection and just be willing to take the chance of being true to yourself regardless of outcome. However, if you get lost in the chase, or you get stifled by fear, chances are you will not be aware of what is truly best for you. You will only be aware of the one possibility to which you've shackled yourself, and subsequently, with which you may be limiting yourself.

Understand that being detached is not the same as being indifferent, because passion is important. It's simply a matter of knowing the difference between being focused and persistent, and being pushy and desperate.

But how can you be persistent and detached from outcome all at the same time? Well, simply live in the moment, enjoy what you're doing, and take inspired action without trying to force things to be a certain way, or worrying over how they will turn out.

You do not need to bully your way through life. You do not need to step over others or push to get your way. Force is not ambition; it's desperation. It's fear and insecurity. When a person is truly comfortable in their own skin, and truly confident in their beliefs and abilities, they do not feel the need to manipulate or force anything.

When we try to manipulate life it is only because we do not have faith in ourselves or in the Infinite Wisdom from which we came. We do things to get approval and we justify our actions based on our fears and doubts rather than any real truth. But if we simply let go a little and learn to detach ourselves from our fears and insecurities we will soon realize that manipulation is not necessary. We will soon realize that what we desire to express will manifest much more easily and joyously if we stay true to ourselves, detach from our desperation, and embrace faith, purpose, and trust instead.

Attachment to outcome is often motivated by our fear of the unknown and our need to control it. By determining and enforcing a specific outcome we satisfy our egos, and this causes us to temporarily feel more secure. But this is not real security, and as such, it can easily get derailed by a simple change in plans or circumstances.

Know that you do not need to figure it all out right now. You do not have to do it all alone. There is an Infinite Energy that is available to you at all times. But when you have blinders on you cannot recognize what is being offered to you in the moment. So instead of closing yourself off from the positive flow of life, why not allow yourself room for flexibility and guidance? You truly have nothing to lose.

Can you honestly say with no doubt whatsoever that you are fully aware of the bigger picture right now; that you are conscious of every step that will ever be? I would wager that you aren't. Because of this, you must relinquish some control over what you think is best for you. You must trust in the bigger picture and understand that there can still be some pertinent information and details that may surface of which you are not yet aware. This is not to say you needn't follow your intuition, for we all have a sixth sense that is very valuable and useful to us. Rather, just make sure that your insecurities and impatience are not deciding what is best for you, but instead, that your higher knowledge is.

In order to recognize what is driving you, simply be conscious of your motives. Are they coming from a pure place of expression, or are they being fed by insecurities, fears, and the need for approval? Are you attached to external things or outcomes, thinking they alone will make you happy? Or do you understand that true happiness comes from within and is then expressed on the outside as a reflection of your inner bliss?

When you are aware of and living in the present moment you are more aware of what's driving you. As such, you are better able to let go of your attachments, go with the flow, and allow yourself to be gently guided to the path that's best. You also no longer feel the need to predict the next hundred steps ahead of time. And while you may have your ideas as to what you want to happen, you can still be open and aware of what's going on in the moment and move with flexibility and trust.

Detaching yourself from the outcome of things is simply a matter of having implicit trust that all is working out for the best. It's not about losing your passion or drive to grow, expand, and succeed. It's simply about letting go of your desperation and trusting that The Universe has your back, as long as you are aligned with it and allowing it to do its thing for you. It's about surrendering your desires to something bigger than yourself and allowing Source Energy to joyously drive you to where you need to be.

Now, it's easy to give up your attachment to things when you don't care about them too much. But how do you let go of your attachment to something when you desire it with such intensity and passion?

Know the difference between passion and desperation. Feel like you're already fulfilled rather than waiting for something to fulfill you. Be in a having state of mind rather than a lack consciousness. Drop your desperation. Act out of faith and certainty. Let go of your personal timelines and specifics of how you think things "should" happen. Trust in Divine Guidance. Trust in your higher-self. Stop pushing and start paying attention to what you really want underneath it all. Trust in your purpose and path. Trust in your higher interests. Then you will enable yourself to freely express the essence of what you desire in infinitely joyous ways, and in ways that are best suited to you. But how do you know the difference between desperation and passion?

Desperation feels like lack and wanting to fill a void. Passion, on the other hand, feels like a desire to express something you love and know is yours in essence already. For instance, you can want a specific job really badly and be desperate about it because you think it's the only one for you. Or you can be genuinely passionate about expressing your talents and being graciously compensated for them all the while knowing there are infinite possibilities to tap into. When you are desperate and attached your primary feelings are of insecurity and impatience. But when you are passionate you are patient, you are enthusiastic, you trust the flow of life, and you are able to surrender your desires in order to manifest what is truly best for you.

Detachment from the Outcome

So the next time you want something, ask yourself if you are feeling desperate about it or excited. This way you'll know the difference between passion and desperation. If you are desperate, you will feel some sort of neediness or lack that you'll want to fill. But if you are passionate, it will just feel good and inspired. You will simply feel certain, detached, enthusiastic, and positive.

Desire is not the enemy. It's attachment that hurts us. Really, what causes misery and despair is the feeling of neediness, desperate craving, and lack. Conversely, when a desire is authentic, it's simply an expression of the purpose you came here to fulfill. And if you look at your desires from the perspective of already having them in essence within you, versus lacking them, you will feel enthusiastic rather than desperate every time.

So feel that you have. Know that you have. Appreciate what you have. Then expand from there. Expand from a feeling of having rather than not having, and more of what you love will be magnetized to you.

What you truly want is already yours. It's already a given. You "ask" via your energy and The Universe delivers. All you need to do is release your resistance and allow yourself to receive what you have been "asking" for. And you do this by letting go of your impatience, doubt, and fear, as well as your need for things to go the way you want them to go. When you let go of your attachments to the how, what, when, and where, you end up allowing yourself to be joyously guided by The Universe; and The Universe knows the exact perfect time, place, and circumstances that are best and most fulfilling for you and all concerned. The Universe always delivers in a win-win manner.

From a place of trust and patience, take action "as if" what you desire is already a given, because in essence, it is. Take the preparatory steps in faith, releasing your attachments and agendas, as well as schedules and specifics. Act on the specifics with which you are inspired, but always leave room for flexibility. Just focus on the essence you love and desire to express as a part of you right now, and do what you can in the moment that is most aligned with that essence. Then let go and allow Divine Intelligence to work it all out.

Letting go of your attachments is really about trust. When you trust in Divine Order you release the need to control or predict all the circumstances of your life. While it can certainly be productive to set intentions, the last thing you want is to manifest something that's simply not right for you. So set your intentions but then let go of them. Let your good flow to you naturally as is best without trying to force, push, or manipulate it. That way you will ensure that what is best will manifest, rather than just what your ego wants.

It can be difficult sometimes to distinguish between what your ego wants and what's truly authentic to you. So how do you know if a desire is aligned with your core, and subsequently right for you? Well, simply by letting go of your attachment to it. Remember, you're not giving up on your desire; you're just giving up your desperation surrounding your desire.

Know that if something is authentic and within your purpose to manifest, being frustrated and attached to it will only push it farther away. And if it's not authentic or within your purpose to manifest, you'll end up wasting your energy thinking about it, and in the process, delaying or preventing what is right for you from appearing. If you let it go, though, then you will know. If you let it go, then you will free yourself to manifest what is truly best for you.

So release your resistance by releasing your desperate wanting of a specific outcome. Then, from your alignment with your authentic self at your core, you will be able to let go and trust The Universe to deliver what's best and most fulfilling for you. You'll be able to surrender your desires and trust in Divine Guidance.

Understand that to truly know if something is right for you, you have to be willing to let go of it, or rather, your desperate wanting of it. This is because the more desperate you are, the more confused you get about what's true and what's not. But when you are able to detach yourself from what you want, you can then see clearly not only as to whether or not you actually want it and why, but also as to what action steps may be needed in order to align you with what you love.

Detachment from the Outcome

When a desire arises, ask yourself why you truly want it, and then let go of it. Understand that pushing, forcing, and moving against the joyous flow of life will eventually end up frustrating you, either by delaying what's yours to come, or by bringing you something unsatisfactory. So instead, relax and let go and you will be allowing what's best to unfold.

Detachment is really about letting go of your ego's fear of the unknown. You don't need to set strict timelines for your intentions thinking it will put pressure on them to manifest. You don't need to fear that if you don't lay it all out in detail covering all the when's and how's and what's that nothing will happen. Understand that you ultimately attract based on your thoughts, feelings, beliefs, alignment, and purpose, and that the specifics will come out of that.

We'll talk more about specifics and timelines up ahead, but for now, know that focusing on specifics can be helpful, but only if you are able to detach from them. Use specifics to help you believe in possibilities and to help you cultivate the feelings behind what you desire, but do not enforce them as strict conditions.

Understand that being attached to specifics can create urgency, desperation, and feelings of "wanting" versus "having," which can then halt the manifestation of what you truly desire altogether. By being attached to specific timing and circumstances it paves the way for potential disappointment to ensue, not to mention stress and pressure to make things happen as per schedule.

The need to set timelines and specifics for our desires is often an expression of the ego anyway. The ego needs to know when and how things will happen because it is motivated by fear, doubt, impatience, and the need to control. When the ego is on unfamiliar ground and facing something unknown, it rushes to make it known, even if that "knowledge" is riddled with illusions. But your true self already knows what it needs to know; it knows that you are already whole and complete right now. If you can just allow yourself to trust in a timing and order that comes of your purpose, you will feel at peace and capable of achieving in essence anything you set out to be, do, and have.

While you can certainly set up to-do lists and schedules for yourself on the things you can control and the action steps you know to take, it's best to allow the rest to just unfold naturally. Go ahead, set your intentions, visualize your desired outcomes, and take inspired action, just do it all with a joyous surrender that allows for flexibility and wonder.

In truth, you do not need to control anything. You simply need to allow the best to unfold naturally. Trust that as you focus on your alignment with your authentic self you will actually have more control over your life than if you just focus on controlling the specifics. Be in the moment, do what you do, but then release your need to figure it all out right now. Just be. Just do. Just flow.

However, as you flow, be sure not to keep tabs on the results you get. Meaning, if you take a leap of faith expecting the best to manifest, be patient because the results you seek may or may not happen immediately. Events will certainly be set in motion, but results may come at varying times and in varying ways. However, doubt will likely hamper your manifestation process, so stay faithful and know that The Universe is functioning on the perfect timeline for you, which may differ from your concept of when and how things "should" happen. There may still be circumstances that need to align of which you may not yet be aware. So keep the faith and follow the proactive cues of The Universe. Keep focusing on the positives. Then the essence you seek will manifest in the best and most fulfilling ways. Stay present and you will naturally release the struggle that comes of being attached to outcome.

Remember, detaching from the outcome is not about giving up on your dreams. You can still take action on what you want to experience while at the same time being detached from the outcome. All you need is trust and faith. Know that you can have an intention, follow through on it, and be detached from it all at the same time simply by living in the moment and trusting in the bigger picture. Know that you can enjoy the essence of what you love right now, fully expect the best, and then manifest total joy as a result.

Detachment from the Outcome

APPLICATION:

Think of something you really want. Is this something you have been chasing after or trying to force? Are you constantly thinking about it as something that's far off into the future? When you think of your desire, do you feel yourself desperately wanting it, or do you feel yourself already having it in spirit? Are you flexible on the package in which it will arrive, or are you stubborn about the specifics? Are you open to something else showing up, something better perhaps?

One way to detach from the outcome is to think of the essence you want to express, instead of focusing only on the specifics you desire to manifest. For instance, you may want more money, but underneath that what you really want is the essence of security, fulfillment, freedom, satisfaction, and so on. Perhaps you want a fitter body, but underneath that you want more self-esteem, confidence, and an overall sense of well-being. So focus on the essence of that right now. Feel the feeling of that right now, regardless of outer appearances.

Let go of the specifics of how and when you will achieve these things, because they are not as important at this time. Don't worry about what will be or how it will be. Just be in the essence feeling of what it is you want, and enjoy that feeling now. Find ways to appreciate yourself and what you have right now. Focus on the attributes in your life that feel good, and then expand from there. It's much more fun and productive to come from a place of love than a place of lack. And when you do come from a place of love, you receive the inspiration you need to help it all manifest. Trust that all is working out perfectly, even if you don't know the specifics of it at this time. Just know that this essence is already within you and that this essence is what will ultimately manifest for you as is best.

Know that you can certainly work out some of the possible logistics and action steps in order to appease your rational mind, in order to get you into a place of believing, and to get you moving on your goals, but remember to also let go of any attachments you might have. Do your best and then let go of the rest.

Do your best not to focus on the manifestation of what you desire. Instead, focus on the essence of having it, because if you're focused on the manifestation aspect alone, you will be indicating a feeling of lack rather than a feeling of abundance. That is, if you're desperate about wanting something, your feeling will be indicative of not having it.

The point of feeling the essence is to understand that this essence is already yours and that your thoughts and feelings surrounding this essence are what propel your manifestations to occur. These manifestations do not occur as something separate from you. They occur as extensions of you. So feel the essence now and let go. Go about your business while still staying aligned in your thoughts, feelings, beliefs, and actions, and then affirm that The Universe is synchronizing everything perfectly on your behalf.

Your alignment with the truth is where your focus needs to be because everything else will flow from there. Focusing on manifestation alone can end up sabotaging the very thing you want to manifest, either by pushing it away through your desperation, or by manifesting it as something ego-inspired, and as such, something you don't really want after all.

So stay focused on your alignment and then when you feel inspired to do so, take your first action step, whatever that is, and fully focus on it, appreciating it as its own opportunity and experience. Do not dwell on where you think this step will take you. Just be fully present with it and enjoy it. Then do this again with the next step and the next one, etc. One step at a time you will not only reach your desired destination, you will also have enjoyed each step along the way.

When it comes to manifesting a specific goal you can certainly have it in mind, thinking about how it would feel to have it as your reality right now. Just remember to refrain from worrying about it, feeling a lack of it, or feeling desperate about it. Detach from the outcome, detach from your need to know how and when it will be. Just enjoy and appreciate what you are doing now and make it as fun and light as possible. See the opportunities embedded within your present moments. Appreciate them for what they are rather than glossing over them on your way to somewhere else.

Detachment from the Outcome

Know that just because you are detached from an outcome this doesn't mean that you can never get excited or enthused about anything. You can still be passionate about something and detached from it at the same time. Simply feel the essence of what you want as yours already. Then feel enthused and satisfied knowing that this truth is manifesting in the best ways and in the best time.

The key is to feel you already have in essence what you desire to express. Then you can feel passionate about it while also being detached from it. Understand that when you feel that you have something, you are not feeling desperate to get it. So know and feel that you do indeed have it within you to manifest what you love. Feel the essence of this truth as your reality right now. Notice the evidence of this truth in your life right now. Be creative with your observations and you will see that the essence you seek is truly already all around you as an expression and extension of you.

This is what it means to be detached from the outcome. It means you are patient, faithful, and trusting that all is well, despite outer appearances, and as such, you can relax and let go into the moment without having any doubts whatsoever. It means you know that you are already connected to everything you desire to express, and that through this connection you will manifest the best outcomes in the best ways, always.

When you relax into the present moment and detach from the outcome you allow what you truly desire to manifest because you are no longer harboring resistance to it. By giving up the chase you give up the struggle as well, but this does not mean that you give up faith. You are not giving up on your dreams, goals, or intentions. You are simply giving up on what's not working for you, and then choosing to be flexible and open to what will.

Finally, make sure you are not tricking yourself into thinking that you are not attached to outcome when really you are. Ask yourself, "How would I truly feel if I didn't get the exact outcome I wanted?" Don't dwell on this thought; just use it to gauge your level of true detachment. Your answer will help you see if you are indeed detached from outcome, or simply fooling yourself into believing that you are. Once you're sure, you can then drop your agendas and truly detach and take action with total faith and surrender.

Meditation:

Think of something you feel you've been chasing after for some time. This can be money, a job, a relationship, a new house, a new car, new friends, a "perfect body," or anything else you feel you've become desperate about having. Now close your eyes, and as you think about this person, thing, or circumstance, take a deep breath, shrug your shoulders, clench your muscles, and feel the tension within your body. Hold this tension for a count of 5.

Now exhale and let go, relax all your muscles and as you do, feel your desire relaxing as well. Feel yourself releasing your tight grip on what you want. Feel your desire going out into the cosmos, trusting that it, or something even better, will manifest in its own time and in the best ways for you. What does that feel like? What does it feel like to no longer have that pressure of needing to achieve this desire of yours? Now focus on what it would feel like to finally have, rather than want, what you truly desire.

Next, ask yourself, "What would happen if I just gave up the desperate chase right now? Would I survive? Would I still exist? Would my world literally come crashing down all around me?" Think about why you're feeling so desperate in the first place. Know that this desperation is not necessary. Know that if you relax your tight grip for just a moment you will realize the best way to manifest the essence of what you truly love.

More often than not when you give up your desperation you will realize that you are just fine as you are; that you have an Infinite Pool of Happiness already within you. You will suddenly come to acknowledge how much you already have to be grateful for right now. You will realize that it's not the end of the world if you don't yet physically have what it is you want. You will realize that everything you need will come to you in its own time, and that if something is truly right for you, it will be. You will realize that you already have within you, not only the essence of what you desire, but also the capability of manifesting it into your life with ease and joy. And from this realization you will be able to take inspired action on your dreams without all the needless attachments. You will finally be able to move forward with trust and faith rather than desperation and force.

Chapter 15:
Fully Engaged

Your life awaits your attention. Are you willing to give it?

Being fully engaged in the moment is a great way to dissolve the stress in your life. Unfortunately, we have become very greedy with our time, and as a result, we've also become more disjointed with our attention. And when our attention is too scattered, we end up doing what appears to be a lot without really getting much done at all. We jump from task to task, never fully committing to the moment at hand, and then we wonder why we feel so stressed.

Stress often comes when we feel overwhelmed with everything we have to do. Our minds become scattered in the attempt to fit everything into what seems to be a small amount of time. But when we get really present in each moment and ground ourselves in appreciation, that's when the stress starts to melt away. When we are fully engaged in this way we are able to find peace. And instead of feeling disconnected and spread too thin, we are able to feel whole again.

Being fully engaged simply means being fully committed to whatever you are experiencing in the present moment. In doing so you end up enhancing the quality of your experience, and you become more aware of the inspiration and guidance that's available to you.

Being fully engaged does not mean you're oblivious to everything else around you. It simply means you are committed to appreciating the present moment and you are willing to give it your full primary attention. At the same time, it is also important to be flexible and available if your attention is needed elsewhere. Being fully engaged, then, is really about maintaining a delicate balance between being focused and open to change at the same time. But no matter where your focus lies, or when it shifts, you need to take your commitment with you. So each time your focus shifts, make sure you are fully engaged and committed to that new moment.

Being fully engaged means noticing when your attention wanders and being able to decide where you want it to go. In this way you become empowered with choice. It's a tall order to ask you to monitor your focus 24/7, but it's not about that. It's about becoming more aware than you are right now and then growing your awareness from there. It's about getting into the habit of being conscious and engaged in as many moments as you can. Sure your mind may wander, but at least your aim will be to keep it focused on authentic joy and fulfillment as much as possible. You may need to remind yourself on occasion to get back into the moment, but it's well worth the effort.

Being fully engaged does not mean being so enthralled in the moment that you lose perspective of the effects of your actions. It is not about instant gratification and a play now, pay later mentality. Engagement is about an awareness of the present moment and a knowing that this moment, and the commitment you put into it, will actually affect the quality of what you get out of it.

Being fully engaged does not mean being overly intense or stressed-out either. It means being present enough with whatever you are doing so that you can fully enjoy the moment you are in right now. It means being committed but not consumed.

When you are committed to the moment you are better able to enjoy and appreciate the task at hand without being bogged down with stress or worry. However, when you are not committed, you are split, i.e. your focus is split out of impatience and the desire for instant gratification, which then results in frustration and burn-out. So learn to have patience and to prioritize what you need to do. This will help you be engaged in what you choose to do. Your primary focus will then naturally gravitate to what matters most to you in each moment.

Fully Engaged

The purpose of life is truly to enjoy each moment. When you prioritize what's most important to you and you decide on the types of experiences you would like to have, you can then choose to align your focus to match. Fully engaging simply means understanding and choosing what you truly love. It means being aligned with your true self and allowing your naturally positive focus to reveal itself. It's a matter of focusing on quality and integrity. It's about enjoying your life to the max rather than just going through the motions.

When you know the essence of what you want to experience in life, it's then up to you to align with that essence and fully engage in it. So align with your core passions and purpose and you will bring forth the true fulfillment you seek. Your focus will naturally gravitate to what you love and you will see the value and opportunity each moment holds. Know that it is through your engagement, understanding, and commitment to the essence of what you love in each moment that you draw forth into your life the fulfillment that is your destiny.

APPLICATION:

Before you do anything, ask yourself, "What kind of life do I want to live?" By asking yourself this question you will start to define your priorities and values in life. This in turn will make it easier for you to get engaged within each moment because you will be doing so with conscious intention and awareness.

Once you've defined in general terms what it is that you want out of your life, the next step is to start with today. Make a list of what you need to get done today and prioritize that list. Once you have prioritized it based on your definition of what's most important to you, make a commitment to put your all into whatever you choose to do in each moment, knowing it's a choice, not an obligation.

For instance, if you have to place a call to a client, put your whole heart and full attention into it. Really listen to what they have to say and truly consider their point of view and needs, not just your own agenda. Make your intention about providing value and sharing knowledge. If you have to buy groceries for your family, take the time to enjoy it, knowing that you are providing nourishment for the ones you love. Be present in the store, notice the fresh produce, how it smells, feels, looks, etc. Make this task about showing love and care for your family, as well as feeling appreciation for everything you have available to you. Whatever your task, make it fun, or at least appreciate it as an opportunity to do something great rather than seeing it as a chore you feel obligated to do.

To ensure that you stay engaged in the moment at hand, keep a journal to jot down any ideas, thoughts, questions, or concerns that come up throughout your day. This journal will help you avoid a wandering mind while you are engaged in something else. You can write down your ideas and then leave them until you are ready to address them further. The point here is to avoid splitting your focus. If you write down your thoughts, your mind will be free to focus on whatever you choose to focus on in that moment, knowing that your notes are safely tucked away and available for you when you are ready to attend to them. Conversely, you can choose to trust that whatever you need to know and whatever you need to remember will come to you when you need it.

To further get you into the habit of engaging in the moment, start by committing to small tasks at first. For example, the next time you're having a meal, use that as a chance to practice your engagement. Appreciate the food you are consuming, appreciate the channels it needed to go through to end up on your plate, savor the flavors, take in the aromas, dwell in the essence you are feeling like comfort, enjoyment, fulfillment, gratitude, and so on. Then continue to practice this way of thinking as your way of being and you will naturally bring quality and fulfillment back into your life.

Being aware of your priorities, making time for what's important to you, and being fully engaged in it, this is the way to be present in all that you do. You can certainly multi-task, but it's best to be mindful as you are doing it, meaning, do not allow your activities to become too robotic. Figure out what's most important to you and then fully engage in that activity when you're in it. Multi-task only if it does not compromise the quality of what you are doing.

As mentioned earlier, being fully engaged does not mean you are oblivious to the world around you. Rather, it's about appreciating whatever you are doing in the moment, while also remaining flexible and capable of shifting focus when it's needed. It's about choosing to be a conscious participant, even when your focus changes, and allowing your consciousness to go with that focus as it changes.

No matter how busy you are you can always find time for what's important to you. The key is to prioritize, make time, and fully engage, yet still be mindful and aware of what's going on around you. The key is to be engaged yet flexible enough to shift your attention when needed. Engaging is more about making conscious choices with your commitment and priorities in mind than it is about being consumed with tunnel-vision. It's about being engaged in and committed to the moment, but not so enthralled that you forget about the other priorities in your life. So be engaged in what you do, but if something else is important to you, make sure you make time for it too.

Being fully engaged does not mean you can never multi-task. If multi-tasking works for you and you can handle the pace without losing out on the quality of your activities, then great, keep doing it. But if you find it challenging and stressful, and if you find that you are ignoring important areas of your life, then practice prioritizing, committing, and putting your attention onto one thing at a time. It's about knowing what's stressful for you and then recognizing where your habits are helping you and where they are hurting you. It's about being aware of what you need to do and then doing something about it.

So make a list of the priorities in your life, things like committing to and being happy with your work, spending enough time with family and friends, giving enough attention to your intimate relationship, eating right, exercising, taking time for yourself, etc. Once you're clear on what's important to you, you will find it that much easier to devote quality time to it. And remember, it truly is more about quality than quantity most times. Don't allow one area of your life to swallow up the others. Remember that being fully engaged in the moment is not about forgetting about everything else. Rather, it's a way for you to find peace and quality in each moment of your life. Be balanced in your commitments. When you're in it, be in it, but also be flexible enough to share your attention with other areas of your life as needed.

Chapter 16:
Taking Inspired Action

Listen to the whispers of your soul and right action will follow.

We live in a very goal-oriented society that places a lot of importance on the actions we perform in our lives. However, what many of us fail to realize is that the consciousness behind our actions is what creates the results we get, not just our actions alone. Action is fine, and often necessary, but action without purpose and heart eventually causes disappointment and struggle in our lives.

When we take action that is motivated by our purpose and by our authentic selves we end up taking action that is inspired. Inspired action, then, is less about doing and more about allowing. It comes from a place of awareness, understanding, and being able to anchor ourselves in the present moment long enough to figure out what's best. It comes from an ability to hear our inner voice and determine the guidance we are being given in each and every moment.

Action that is not inspired is often motivated by fear. As such, it causes us to be impulsive, hasty, and redundant with our choices. We are indeed very habitual beings, often skeptical of things unknown to us. Consequently, when we have doubts, we allow those doubts to dictate our lives, simply because we are too afraid to change our mindset. We let our fear of the unknown stop us from taking action that may be different from what we've grown accustomed to, but this in turn causes us to limit ourselves in what we can accomplish.

Inspired action, however, comes from being able to step out of your fear and into the consciousness of the present moment, using that presence to wipe away all your limits and doubts. Inspired action causes you to step outside the boundaries you've set for yourself, giving you the confidence and courage to chart a new course in a new and better direction.

Inspired action is not about struggling to get what you want in life. Rather, it's about stepping into the flow of things and allowing your purpose to gently and lovingly guide you in your best direction. Inspired action is smart action that takes you away from hardship and moves you towards enjoyment and true fulfillment.

Taking inspired action is about joyously expressing yourself through love and purpose. It's about aligning your thoughts, feelings, beliefs, and actions with the truth of your being, and allowing bliss to flow to you and through you naturally and effortlessly. It's about surrendering to Source Energy and allowing yourself to be guided to what's best for you. You do not need to fight, struggle, force, or chase after anything. You can be persistent, you can be focused, and you can be committed, all the while maintaining a joyous and trusting heart in each moment.

Struggle is not a requirement for success. We often believe that it is, but that's simply due to all the false information we've been handed in our lives, and all those feelings of unworthiness we still have about ourselves. Realize that success can come more easily when you simply align yourself with your Source. But if you believe you must struggle to be happy then it's likely that you will because struggle is actually more a by-product of your faulty beliefs than it is a matter of any real truth or necessity.

Sure, struggle can have its place in teaching you lessons that you may need to learn, but if you can be proactive in your life and bypass the struggle, why not do that? Why not opt for something so much better than struggle? Opt for peace and happiness, opt for ease and joy, and opt for knowing that you are deserving by nature and that all you need to do is align with who you really are and accept total love and bliss as your birthright.

When talking about inspired action we must make a distinction between perseverance and struggle, because too often we mistake one for the other. Perseverance is about believing in yourself and moving past obstacles with

Taking Inspired Action

trust and faith. Struggle, on the other hand, comes from fear and a belief in lack. Struggle comes of force and a resistance to the natural flow of life. When you ignore your purpose, when you discount The Universe as your resource, struggle is what ensues. But when you trust in yourself and when you trust in something bigger than yourself, you can persist with a healthy detachment from the outcome because you know with certainty that all is working out for the best.

Taking inspired action is about taking action in the moment based on a knowing that you can be, do, and have in essence anything you desire. It's allowing yourself to act with certainty by feeling the experience you desire to manifest as your true reality right now, in your heart, mind, and soul. It's about filling your heart with appreciation for all that you have now, and all that you know is possible too. It means being confident in your certain success, and trusting completely in Divine Timing and Order.

Inspired action can be defined as action that's taken out of joy, confidence, and faith. It always leads you down the best path and never causes you to regret your decisions, no matter what the outcome. Inspired action is proactive and guided and gives you the confidence to move forward on what you love with commitment and follow-through.

However, while inspired action is the best way to go, it's important to point out that as you are learning to listen to your inner voice, it might take you a little while to distinguish the voice of your higher-self from that of your ego. So as you learn, you mustn't become shy to take action out of fear that your actions may not yet be fully inspired. You cannot use your fear of failure as an excuse for not taking any action at all because that will likely lead you down a path of procrastination and subsequent stagnation.

Ideally you would be so attuned to your intuition and guidance that your awareness would lead you to take the inspired action that's best. But what if you're not quite clear on the message yet? Indeed, sometimes it's better to work with what you know of in the moment than it is to wait for conditions to be "perfect." After all, perfection is all about perception anyway. Who's to say conditions aren't perfect as they are right now? Maybe this is the jumping off point? This does not mean jumping into something impulsively or doing something that you thoroughly dislike. It simply means being willing to act even if you aren't sure of the outcome, all the while trusting that no matter what happens, it will somehow take you to where you need to be. It's about taking a leap of faith and knowing that the next step will show up exactly when you need it to.

Do not wait for conditions to improve before taking action. Improve the conditions by getting out there and taking action "as if" the essence of what you want is already in motion. Know that no matter what decision you make, at least it will be moving you forward in life. One way or another you will learn what you need to learn. So do your best to make conscious choices, but then let go of your worries and attachments and trust in the bigger picture.

Do not let fear trick you into playing the waiting game. If you do, you could end up allowing your life to pass you by. Certainly do what feels right to you, and if waiting feels good to your soul then that's what may be best. Just don't be swayed by fear and insecurity as this can cause you to make hasty decisions. You need to learn the language of your soul so that you know what is truly inspired and what is not.

Distinguishing between what's inspired and what's not may require practice, so if you want to know the difference, figure it out through experience. In order to know how your inner self talks to you, you must be willing to make mistakes. This doesn't mean you will, it just means you must no longer fear it. When you set yourself free from fear in this way you become more open and more aware when guidance does appear.

Inspiration can come in many forms. You may be inspired right now and not even know it. Maybe the answer you seek is staring you right in the face. But if you are too afraid to ask questions and if you are too afraid to look for answers, you will never really know where your full potential can take you. Understand that taking inspired action is really about acting with curiosity, awareness, certainty, and surrender in each moment, even if you don't know all the details at the forefront.

No matter what action you take, trust that you will learn something about yourself as a result. Do not fear failure because failure is really just a lesson on how to do it better the next time around. But when you don't take action you may end up wondering, "What if?" You may end up stuck in your same patterns of mediocrity. Being afraid of failure will never get you to where you want to be. Obviously we all want to get it right the first time, but we mustn't fear making mistakes. We mustn't fear failure. We must embrace life as an adventure and know that no matter what, we will be ok.

Inspired action is about maximizing your chances of right action; action that is aligned with your true calling and true happiness. Inspired action is about creating a balance between inspiration, contemplation, and follow-through. Do not allow fear to stop you from moving through these phases with joy and confidence. Think, plan, and do, but most of all, allow yourself to receive the joy that is already yours.

Inspired action is purpose-driven, and when you learn to hear the voice of your inner guide, this is when you become confident in your inspirations. This is when your actions become about ease and flow and alignment with your true self. Understand that inspired action is about allowing your good to come forth. It's about being your authentic self. It is not about struggle or hardship.

Know that inspired action will always be authentic and true to your soul. So release your fears, follow your intuition, and then take inspired action in the moment with what you authentically love, and all that you truly desire will flow to you with ease.

Vulnerability Redefined:

When we decide to take action on something, often a part of us hesitates due to the vulnerability factor, i.e. we fear rejection, we fear being hurt, and we fear being disappointed. But being afraid gets us nowhere.

Let's look at some common descriptions of vulnerability: susceptible, weak, defenseless, helpless, exposed, in danger, at risk, and in a weak position.

No wonder we're so scared of vulnerability, with these descriptions, who wouldn't be?

Vulnerability insinuates being unprotected and at risk. And this is exactly how we can feel when we open ourselves up to someone or something at the risk of being rejected, judged, or hurt. But without this risk we end up staying closed and unhappy. So what do we do?

We must change our perception of vulnerability. So instead of seeing yourself as being vulnerable, see yourself as willing to take a chance, even if the outcome differs from what you had hoped. Simply be open.

Yes, it's true, inspired action is based on openness. But you do not need to feel defenseless or weak or in danger as a result. There really is no need to be on guard, defensive, cold, or closed-off. The only reason you might feel this way is out of fear of being hurt and disappointed. But there truly is nothing to fear.

Being open in spite of your fears makes you strong. "Vulnerability," in this case, is not a sign of weakness at all. And even if there is a risk of being rejected or judged, you still need not feel vulnerable because you know you are whole as you are, and that nothing can ever change that. As such, you do not need anyone's approval and you can be ok with whatever outcome may come.

It's not that you no longer care. It's just that you no longer fear. You may get hurt, but so what? You'll live, you'll learn. If you realize that everything is ultimately for your benefit anyway, the risk won't seem so grave. All you really fear here is the bruising of your ego. But your true self is what matters most. You already know the truth of your worth at your core so there really is no need to fear.

So instead of fearing vulnerability, see yourself as open. Because when you are open you are real, you are fearless, and you are able to do what you need to do. You are able to act in spite of your fears because you know your fears are just illusions anyway. You are able to take the risk of being open with your feelings, realizing that it's really no risk at all because no matter the outcome, you'll be just fine, you will learn from it, and you will get the best out of it.

Being open does not need to put you at risk. In fact, it is when you close yourself off from opportunities that you are really at risk; at risk for living a mediocre life. Know that there is no real risk because ultimately any outcome will lead you to your best outcome. So be yourself, no matter the outcome, and go forward being yourself without apology and without regret.

When you can be real and not put on defenses or put up walls, that takes strength and confidence. If you can be true and real and authentic and not worry about outcome or approval and just take a chance, you will be well on your way to living your greatest life. And you will feel good in the process because you will know that you did all that you could do.

Being willing to feel vulnerable and not fearing rejection or disappointment, and taking a chance as a result, leaves you open to receiving what you love. But playing it safe only keeps you in a false sense of security. And what does "playing it safe" mean anyway? Keeping your ego appeased? Know that when you can stop worrying about getting approval you will finally liberate yourself to be limitless and fearless. Know that you are always safe and protected. Understand that it's only your ego that feels vulnerable, in which case, so what? You can get over that.

Taking Chances:

Inspired actions are based on taking chances in life. But because they are backed by faith and trust, in truth, they are not really that risky to begin with. Taking a chance is much better than wondering "what if" all your life. At least it's a move forward. And even if in retrospect your action felt like it was a mistake, at least you can now learn from it and do better as you progress. So laugh it off. At least you made an effort and took a chance.

It's fun and liberating to take proactive chances. It's fun to see how things work out. It's fun not being so serious about everything, and instead, lightening-up a bit. It's liberating to trust in Divine Order and know that ultimately all is for the best. It's fun to know that actions lead to results. But if you don't take the chance, you'll possibly never know what could have been.

When you take a chance you can be proud of yourself for taking one step forward towards the fulfillment of your best dreams. Even if the outcome turns out to be different from what you wanted, at least you can find comfort in knowing that you are moving forward with your life rather than being stuck in old negative patterns. Taking a chance means stepping outside of your comfort zone, and as a result, surpassing those negative patterns that obviously do not serve you well.

It's so liberating to no longer worry about getting approval, making mistakes, being rejected, or feeling vulnerable. It's a much more fun and peaceful way to live. It's liberating to be trusting, optimistic, positive, and enthusiastic about life and no longer worry over outcomes. It's liberating to let go of the doubt and to believe in possibilities.

Taking chances is about releasing your fear that what you want isn't possible for you. So when you want something, be sure not to discount it by thinking it will never, or can never be. By doing so you may think you're protecting yourself from hurt and disappointment, but really all you're doing is sabotaging yourself. When you think, "Hey, there is a possibility for this to manifest," what you are doing is letting go of your resistance, which allows what you desire, or something even better, to manifest in your life. And know that no matter how slight it may seem, there is always a possibility that your best dreams can come true.

Take the chance because somehow it will lead you to where you need to go anyway. At least you will be moving forward rather than stuck in procrastination and fear of failure. One way or another you'll learn about what to do next. But also know that taking chances is not about being impulsive, reckless, or reactive. Rather, it's about following your internal guidance system and taking positive and inspired action in spite of your fears.

Enjoy the ride. Release the pressure. Take proactive risks and have fun with it. See your life as an adventure. Don't worry about making mistakes. Be excited to learn, trust in your guidance, and then just go for it.

Taking Inspired Action

Don't get caught up in a need for instant gratification. Rather, be patient and don't prematurely judge something as a "failure." Stay with it a while longer because your success may be just around the corner. In fact, you are already a success just by having taken inspired action in the first place.

Don't be so hard on yourself either. Relax your expectations of yourself and of others. As you do, you will naturally feel more encouraged to take proactive risks, and in doing so, you will reach your goals without all the stress and anxiety. Let go of some of the control and trust in something bigger. Then you'll be able to take proactive chances with confidence and an optimistic outlook on life.

Taking chances is about releasing your need for approval, and as such, being able to ask for what you need and want without fearing that others won't like you for it or perceive you as being difficult. Don't worry about maintaining a certain image. Do what you feel is right in the moment and don't look back. Leave your fear of embarrassment and disapproval at home. You don't need it. Move forward using all your choices, all your lessons, all your blunders, and all your successes to propel you to take even more chances in your life on the path to fulfilling your best dreams.

Jump out of your comfort zone. Know that you can do it. Know that every time you do you will be building more and more confidence within yourself. You can start with baby steps and build your confidence from there. The important thing is not necessarily how big your leaps are, but the fact that you are taking them in the first place.

Taking chances is based on having faith. So don't over-analyze. You don't need to figure everything out right away. You'll know what you need to know as you need to know it. Don't procrastinate or fear failure or making mistakes. Do it anyway. Have fun with it.

Really, don't be afraid to fail. Failure is just another type of result anyway, which may actually lead you to something great. So there really is nothing to lose or fear. Be proud of yourself for just making the attempt.

Do it anyway. Push through your fear. You can take it. It's no big deal.

You Are Here

It's better than letting fear control you. And by going for it, you'll end up overcoming your fears once and for all. Now isn't that the best reward?

When you do take a chance, know that you cannot be wishy washy about it. If you procrastinate or bounce back and forth too much it will only psych you out even more. So be decisive. Just decide and go for it. At least it's a move forward. And, the more decisive you are, the more you will learn the voice of your soul. And the more you learn the voice of your soul, the more attuned you will be to your higher guidance and the inspired actions that are best for you.

Enjoy the ride. Release the pressure. Take chances and have fun with them. Don't worry about outcomes or making mistakes. Be excited and enthused and trust in your higher-self. Move forward with confidence knowing that ultimately you'll get to the place that's best. In the meantime, enjoy the journey of it. See it as a fun adventure. Let go of your expectations and just roll with it, being content at the very fact that you are taking action on your best dreams. Everything has its reason so trust in that too. Do your best to line up with your truth and then let yourself go into the flow of things. Trust your guidance to carry you to where you need to be.

And remember, taking chances is not about regretting your decisions after the fact if they didn't go as planned. Taking a chance is about knowing that when one door closes, another one opens, but that you need to stop lingering on the closed door and start looking for the openings if you're going to manifest what you truly love.

Taking Inspired Action

APPLICATION:

Whenever you feel doubtful about what to do next, simply get quiet for a moment and pose the question in your mind. Listen for that quiet voice that guides you. It may feel weird at first if you are not yet accustomed to asking for guidance, but if you have a little faith you will realize that you are connected to an Infinite Pool of Knowledge that is always available to you.

If nothing comes to you at first, don't get discouraged. It is often when we let go of our need to know that we get the inspiration we seek. Simply pose the question and then just let it be. Go about your business and just be open to receiving an answer. Everyone and everything is a messenger so be open and aware but don't be overly analytical or paranoid. Instead of obsessing over the answer, just pose your question and let it go. Know that your answer can come in an infinite amount of ways, like through a great idea, a dream, a conversation, a thought, a feeling, a song, etc. Be open to synchronicities without brushing them off as mere coincidences, but do not jump to conclusions either.

In order to be able to read signs properly you must be willing to let go of your ego's concept of what a true sign really is. Meaning, we often see and perceive things as we want to see and perceive them. It's a little trick the ego plays on us. We read into things that really aren't there simply because we want them to be there. So, to avoid misjudging the guidance you receive, let go of your personal agendas as much as possible and aim to stay neutral. Be ok with any outcome, trusting that whatever the outcome, it will be the best outcome for you. With this attitude you will be much better able to accurately interpret the guidance you receive.

When you do get inspired with an authentic desire or idea, don't be afraid to take action on it now. In the bigger picture there really are no such things as "mistakes." There are only learning opportunities. So don't be afraid to act because you're afraid of making a mistake. Know that what may feel like a mistake can also be perceived as a learning experience and a lesson for what not to do in the future. What may seem like a mistake in the moment can also actually be the right path, only you're not aware of it just yet.

When we get attached to a specific outcome, that often leads us to misinterpret the results we get. Instead, have patience and trust that all of the pieces will come together in the right time and ways. Trust in the bigger picture, trust that all is working out for the best in one way or another, and trust that you will know what's what in due time.

So if it feels right and you feel confident that your motivation is coming from an authentic place, then take action; take a chance. Don't worry about what the next steps will be. Just do what you know to do in this very moment and trust that the next step will reveal itself when the time is right. Don't try to figure out the meaning or outcome of everything, as this may lead you to over-analyze and procrastinate. Take action and let the way reveal itself to you, one step at a time.

If you are unsure of when or if to take action, ask yourself these questions: "If all my fears and doubts no longer existed, would I take action on this or not?" "What's stopping me?" "What am I afraid of?" If you are honest with your answers, you will know what to do.

Understand the difference between a gut instinct and an ego fear. For example, notice if what's stopping you is a deep nudge from within, often one that you can't quite explain, or if it's your fear of failure, disappointment, or rejection that's causing you to procrastinate. The more you are present with your motives, the more you will understand them, and the more confidence you'll have when you actually do take chances and inspired actions towards your goals.

So think of something right now that you want to do but that you're afraid to do. Are your fears justified? Are you feeling vulnerable, and if so, why? What are you really afraid of? Most often you'll notice that you are more afraid of your ego being bruised than you are about anything real. In this case, realize this fact and then choose an action step that takes you outside of your ego's comfort zone. Choose something proactive, decide to do it, and then take the leap. Open yourself up to the possibilities and detach yourself from the outcome, and then just go for it. More often than not you won't regret it.

Then in general, be lighter about things. Don't be so serious. Don't forget to enjoy yourself because that's what being inspired is all about. Have more fun in your life (proactively of course). Let yourself go with the flow a little more. Then take inspired action, but also relax into it, enjoying your life one moment at a time.

And one more thing, taking inspired action is about noticing where you are not aligned with the truth of who you are, and then doing something to rectify that. It's great to be aware of the areas in your life that need your attention. But if you are not willing to give them that attention, then you might as well not know. It's almost worse to know and not do, than it is to not know at all. So don't just notice the areas of your life and the qualities of yourself that need adjustment. Do something about it. Take inspired action to come into the person you are truly meant to be.

Asking for Affirmative Guidance:

One way to receive the inspiration you seek is to ask for affirmative guidance. When you ask for affirmative guidance you are not placing a passive request or begging or hoping for a change. Instead, you are affirming your guidance, knowing full well that the direction you need is already yours. By "asking" you are simply opening yourself up to receiving. So "ask" with the awareness that you already know. "Ask" with the knowing that the answer is already yours and available to you right now. Know that your "asking" will then be answered simply by virtue of your alignment with the answer, and through your openness to accept it.

Ask not from the perspective of desperation and lack. Ask with confidence and gratitude, knowing that this joyous guidance is not only your birthright, it is also already a part of you. Then let go and let yourself be led without trying to control every detail. Ask, let go, and then take inspired action. It's really that simple. As soon as you get out of your own way by releasing your need to know everything ahead of time, and as soon as you feel confident that your answers are already within you, you will receive, or rather, become aware of the inspiration you seek exactly when and as you need it.

You Are Here

As you await your guidance keep your focus and feelings on being receptive, and then have trust and faith. Do not be wary, doubtful, or impatient. After all, it's the feeling behind your "asking" that will determine the results you get. If you feel doubtful and frustrated, you will likely block your answers. But if you are trusting, faithful, relaxed, and joyful, your answers will become proactively apparent to you.

Chapter 17:
Releasing Negative Judgments

Judgments are a matter of perception. Simply change your perceptions and you'll change the way you experience life.

All too often we make limited judgments about what's good and what's bad, what's right and what's wrong. But the problem with this is that our judgments often come from a very limited understanding of the bigger picture. It's one thing to make assessments, but it's when we pre-judge based on our limited knowledge and projected insecurities that we end up sabotaging ourselves and turning our present moments into something stressful and confusing.

It can sometimes feel intimidating or even scary to be fully present, especially when the present doesn't seem all that appealing. But to deny or reject where we presently are in life only prolongs the circumstances that we don't like, and denies us the opportunity for change.

Our negative judgments of ourselves, of others, and of the circumstances in our lives are derived from our false selves. A lot of the time the judgments we make aren't even our own. They come from years of societal brainwashing, telling us what's good and what's bad and what we "should" or "shouldn't" be doing, and they come from our fears and insecurities too. We worry about what others will think. We fear that we aren't good enough as we are right now. We chase after more hoping that somehow it will make us feel better, happier, and more deserving.

But all of this is a fabrication. There is nothing inherently "wrong" with you. You don't have to chase after anything because you are not really lacking anything. You may have some layers of doubt preventing you from seeing this truth, but these layers only come from fear. These layers of doubt are not who you truly are; they are false blankets of security that prompt you to label yourself and judge yourself based on misguided standards that are often not even your own.

It's important to explain here that by nature you deserve to be happy, you deserve love, peace, prosperity, and all things you consider to be good in life. But what about those who are delinquent or disrespectful towards others, do they deserve goodness too?

Here's the thing, there's a difference between being deserving by nature and being deserving by behavior. The spirit is deserving because it's all about truth. The spirit is one with goodness. Deserving is what you are at your core. However, what you receive is dependent upon your level of alignment with your core. And so, if you put out something negative into the world, as long as you continue that streak of behavior, eventually that's what will be reflected back to you.

There is no punishing deity that hands out reprimands or rewards. What you put out you bring about. No one else and nothing else can truly be held accountable. There is a Source, yes, but this Source gives based on what you "ask" for. And what you "ask" for is based on the energy you put out into the world. What you get are simply results. So understand that while at your core you deserve the best, your behavior must be aligned with that core in order for you to truly receive the best. So ask yourself this: while you are deserving in spirit, is your behavior deserving as well?

Stop thinking in terms of whether or not you are worthy of good in your life, or whether or not you are good enough to receive it. Instead, get present and start paying more attention to your behavioral patterns and the motives behind them, because these will show you where you are aligned and where you have strayed from your core truths.

Then, as you start to understand yourself more, you will be able to accept the present as it is, and accept yourself as you are, thereby releasing the pressure and stress associated with not feeling good enough, smart enough, successful enough, etc. As you release these feelings, your focus will then naturally gravitate to being enough, having enough, and so on. And when you feel like you are enough, you become enough, and the experiences in your life rise up to exemplify that "enoughness."

Understand that the point of life is not to punish yourself for your perceived short-comings, or to dwell on your perceived imperfections. The point of life is to reveal who you truly are. And who you truly are is all good. You are a loving and joyous being that was made of the consciousness of perfection. Understand that perfection is a subjective term; it can mean anything you want it to mean. So if you can accept yourself and the present moment as it stands, then you will be able to see the perfection that lies within you right now.

Sometimes it's hard to see the perfection within. Sometimes all we see are imperfections, not just in ourselves, but in others as well. But by focusing on these perceived imperfections we end up giving them power over our lives. We end up feeding into the false beliefs that created our insecurities in the first place.

The truth is that we all come from a place of perfection and love. We were all made perfect the way we are. And there is a reason why we are the way we are. We are here to develop into our true, powerful selves. We are here to expand and grow into our full potential. We are here to embrace our purpose and our blessings and share them with the world.

We each are a gift to this world, and we've been given many gifts as well. We need to wake up to these gifts, but the longer we are stuck in false thinking, the longer it will take for us to realize why we're truly here. We are here to embrace our similarities and respect our differences. We are here to love and respect ourselves and love and respect others. We are here to serve a great purpose only we can serve. We are not here to be judgmental or punishing.

Keep this in mind before you judge others. Realize that all anyone ever wants is to be happy and loved. Different people go about achieving this in different ways, some more misguided than others. But when you realize that everyone wants in essence what you want, you can see past their veils and see into their souls. Know that everyone has a purpose and everyone has value. You don't have to befriend everyone. Just release your anger and judgment, because when you harbor resentment you not only negatively affect others, you also end up poisoning yourself in the process.

Everyone comes from their own unique vantage point and experience, so instead of getting angry, simply understand that you may not understand. Know that you can accept your differences and communicate your point of view in such a way that allows you to express yourself, while also being able to listen. At the very least you'll be able to agree to disagree. But also keep in mind that there is more than one viable way to get things done. Just because it's not your way doesn't mean it isn't a way. Remember, the concept of "right" and "wrong" is really a matter of perception anyway.

When you are able to shift your perceptions to be more accepting and less judgmental, you will also release your resentment and anger towards other people, towards the circumstances in your life, and even towards yourself. By releasing your need for approval you also end up freeing yourself from stress and disappointment. Understand that someone else's choices, opinions, actions, and standards are their own, not yours. Know that you make your own choices in life, and that you need to take responsibility for those choices, but you do not need to take ownership of another's. You need to forgive, learn, and move on.

When you feel resentful you can bet that you've taken on a victim mentality. But if you realize your own role in it, instead of wasting time blaming and accusing, you can spend your time directing your focus onto better things. It's simple: if you don't feel victimized, you won't feel resentful, and you'll be able to move on that much faster.

It helps to know that the negative behaviors of others are the result of their own need and desire to be loved. They are acting out in the way that they know best to get what they believe they need. It may not be an ideal way, or even "fair" to others, but it's what they know. This doesn't mean you have to tolerate it, excuse it, or even keep quiet about it. Just realize it and you will be well on your way to releasing your own resentment. You may even be able to forgive.

Forgiveness is freeing as it releases you from the hold of others. Know too that you can still hold someone accountable and forgive them at the same time. Forgiveness doesn't mean accepting a person's same behavior over and over again. It's simply a tool you can use to let go of your own anger and make more proactive decisions because of that.

Sure, it's easy to feel angry and disappointed with people and circumstances if/when they don't meet your expectations. But again, you must take responsibility for what you attract into your own life, as this is the only way you will stop negative patterns from re-occurring. Instead of dwelling on the unfairness of others' behavior towards you, which again is really succumbing to a victim mentality, think about why you've attracted this in the first place. What belief of yours is this behavior mirroring? Is it a quality you exhibit as well but haven't noticed? Is there an action you are being prompted to take once and for all that you've been avoiding, like standing up for yourself perhaps? Instead of over-analyzing what he said or what she did, work from the inside-out and you will no longer be at the mercy of the conduct of others, and as such, you will finally be empowered.

Empowerment is really about letting go of whatever doesn't serve you well. In this case, making negative judgments can turn you into a victim, which leaves you helpless. But if you take responsibility for yourself you will no longer feel like a victim of circumstance. Instead, you will feel enabled to take your life into your own hands and shape it as you choose.

Empowering yourself means that you no longer measure yourself against other people's standards. It means that your happiness does not solely depend on things external to you. It also means that you no longer feel the need to negatively judge others or the circumstances in your life because you know that this only gives your power away.

Releasing judgment really means releasing the pressure of how you think things "should be." To accept things as they are is to know that perfection exists in each moment, even if you don't realize it, and that everything has its reason. It's about trusting in synchronicity and in your personal path. It's about knowing that you are gifted with the free will to make all your own choices from moment to moment. By being present and non-judgmental you then open yourself up to recognize the opportunities and blessings that are present in your life right now.

It's funny, if things don't go the way we want them to we automatically assume that things aren't as they "should be." But what does "should be" really mean anyway? If something "is," then it is as it "should be" by the very virtue that "it is." It's there showing you that you're either aligned and on track or misaligned and off track. Everything is here for your ultimate benefit. If things are the way they are then there must be a good reason for it, so in essence, things are as they "should be." This doesn't mean you can't change them. It just means that there's a reason for them, and that you can use this feedback in order to align with what you truly love rather than wasting your time negatively judging "what is."

The key to freedom is really in releasing yourself from false pressures and standards that simply do not serve you. You can do this by getting present in the moment and by realizing that where you are right now is where you need to be right now for your own personal journey. It is where your consciousness has brought you. Whatever the reason, know there is a purpose for it, relax into it, accept it, learn from it, and know you have the power to shift it if you want to by simply releasing it and choosing a different focus; a focus where you are aligned with the truth that you are already whole and complete and one with all you could ever desire.

Release your fears, release your doubts, release your guilt, release your judgments, and feel free to express who you truly are. If you do not feel joy, if you do not feel peace, if you do not feel accepting, know that you are still harboring false beliefs and negative judgments within you. So choose to see yourself for your true self, not all the false judgments, labels, and masks you and/or others have placed upon you.

Releasing Negative Judgments

Don't be so hard on yourself. While introspection is good, it's important not to get carried away with "self-improvement." Life is about growing and learning. It is about expanding and expressing. It is not about making yourself feel so bad that you don't have any energy, motivation, or even confidence left to move forward on your dreams.

Anyway, you don't so much need to "improve" on yourself, as that may imply that there's something wrong or missing from you as you are. It's really about self-awareness and self-empowerment. It's about recognizing that you already have it within you to be all that you want to be. You can certainly expand on your skills and develop new qualities, but know that you're not here to "fix" yourself. You are here to come into your true self, to release your false layers, and to reveal the true perfection that lies within.

On the surface it may sometimes appear that there's something wrong with you or missing from your life, but in actuality, you do not lack anything. You have the ability to be, do, and have in essence anything you desire in life, and it's all within you right now. So think of this process called life as an opportunity to develop yourself into the person you were meant to be, into who you really are at your core, by awakening to the fact that you already are that person right now. Think of it as self-discovery. And as you discover who you truly are, your life will naturally improve as a result simply because it will be reflecting your inner truth.

On your journey you will discover more and more of who you are at your core, but it does not need to happen overnight. You have an opportunity to see the best in yourself and the best in others in every moment. It is a choice you make. And the more you see yourself for who you truly are, underneath all the masks, the more overall fulfillment you will feel in your life.

You are here to learn and express the truth of your being. Simply rid yourself of your misconceptions and you will reveal the perfection of who you really are and what you're truly capable of doing, having, and being. Let go of your negative judgments and you will naturally release the resistance that has been keeping you from the life you love.

APPLICATION:

List as many labels or judgments you can think of that have been placed on you (by others or by yourself). Now look at each one and decide if you are truly defined by these labels or if there is more to you than that. Can you accept that you are not just your job, your title, your weight, your clothes, your net worth, etc? While some labels can undoubtedly describe you in certain aspects of your life, they can also be used to limit you if you let them.

The truth is that although labels are placed on you, these labels do not define the totality of who you truly are. Labels are simply a means by which we try to make sense of things. It's the ego's way of creating order and predictability. Unfortunately, we often allow these labels to completely define, not only who we are, but also what we believe we can be, do, and have.

In order to move past your labels and judgments you must realize that you are infinite, you are dynamic, you are powerful, and you are authentically you. No one can take away who you are at your core. You are always capable of greatness. You are great right now. You can be, do, and have the essence of anything you desire in life because it is always yours to express.

So ask yourself, "Are the labels and judgments I'm using to define my life and who I am working for me or against me?" If you believe that they are not helping you, it's time to change your definitions. Realize that your ultimate value does not depend on the type of car you drive, the clothes you wear, the job you have, or the number of people that approve of you. Your value is inherent. You do not need to prove your worth to anyone. You need only to recognize it, embrace it, and honor it as your truth right now.

Once you've realized that your self-worth and your authenticity come from within, notice others you have judged in the past. Know that they too are great and they too are not defined by their labels. No one can truly judge anyone totally accurately anyway. We can have our opinions, but truly there is so much to each person that to judge is to give into limited thinking and to feed into our own insecurities.

Releasing Negative Judgments

Everyone comes from their own perspectives in life that are likely way more dynamic than your judgments will afford. Just like you wouldn't want to be judged for your perspectives, don't judge others for theirs. We're all doing the best we feel we can in each moment. So release your negative judgments of others and of yourself. And release your need for approval too because at the end of the day, you need to do what's right for you. You need to love yourself beyond what others think about you. And the more content and forgiving you are with yourself, the more compassionate you will be with others too.

So give up your urge to judge, gossip, and make hasty assumptions about other people. Let them be. Know they have the freedom to be unique and authentic, and so do you. Question why you feel the need to judge in the first place, and if it's coming from your own insecurities or feelings of lack or inadequacy. Know that you will never truly build yourself up by tearing others down.

Next time you feel the urge to gossip or judge, stop yourself. If you are around people who gossip, change the subject or move away from the situation. And when you feel the urge to judge yourself as less than adequate, resist that urge as well. Be forgiving with yourself and others and you will find yourself feeling more confident and happier than ever before. Celebrate people's strengths and successes rather than focusing on your limited judgments of them. Because the more you focus on success in general, whether it's yours or another's, the more overall success you will see in your own life.

Respect and enjoy your own uniqueness, and respect and enjoy the uniqueness of others. Accept people as they are, without needing to change them. And accept yourself as you are too. We are all perfect in our own right, only with different degrees of concealment. Learn to see beyond the masks and you will learn to live an authentic and loving life.

Affirm: "I am perfect and whole as I am right now. I accept myself as I am right now, and I accept others as they are as well." This will align you with the truth of your being, and subsequently, it will release you from the blockages that may be standing in the way of your own fulfillment.

Know that we are not all meant to be the same. Find the beauty in our differences and realize that it's a chance to learn more about others and about ourselves. In one way or another, this world is a mirror. To judge others is to judge ourselves.

So take a look at your life right now. What are you unfairly judging? Is it a person, a situation, or yourself? Understand that your judgment is likely founded in limited knowledge at this point. Know that there is a reason for everything and that rushing to judgment may lead you down a misguided path.

Look at your life and the feedback it's giving you. Choose to accept yourself and your life as it is right now, and accept others too. And know that by doing so you will be releasing resistance, thereby allowing what you truly love to come forth into your life. Appreciate your place in your journey right now, and trust that it is moving you closer to revealing your true self. Appreciate each moment for the miracle and blessing that it is, for life in and of itself is a great blessing to be embraced by us all.

Chapter 18:
You Have Already Arrived

Never take for granted where you are right now, for where you are right now, and your attitude about it, will set the tone for where you are going.

Being present is about understanding that you have already arrived somewhere. By the very virtue that you are here, you are somewhere. You are already a "somebody" right now, and valuable just as you are. Constantly striving to be somewhere else or someone else only takes you away from the joy and value of the present moment, and the gifts that lie therein.

You are here right now, so you are somewhere right now. You can spend your entire life running from place to place, but the truth is that your fulfillment starts with where you are right now. This moment has the potential to be great. And you can make it great by choosing a positive perception of it. Your joy, your happiness, your fulfillment all starts with you, right here and right now.

We strive to get somewhere else, we chase after things we think will make us happy, but the truth of the matter is, we are arriving all the time. We are constantly manifesting something, in each moment of every day. But often we are not conscious of where we are or what we are accomplishing or receiving because we are too busy trying to get somewhere else.

Seriously, think about everything you've already manifested today. If you list everything to the last detail you will probably already have a list at least a mile long. You've already had a number of desires fulfilled throughout your day so far. Your desire for clean teeth, your desire for a cup of coffee, your desire for hot water, your desire for a ride to work, your desire for clothing to wear, your desire to breathe, and so on.

So instead of constantly trying to get somewhere else, do your best to appreciate where you are already. Because the way to get somewhere else starts right here and right now. Your choices and your feelings right now are what will determine your future. The appreciation that you feel for wherever you are right now is what will manifest the joy that you will experience next.

Feel appreciation for the moment. Feel appreciation for what you've already manifested. Chances are there have been plenty of things you have been taking for granted in your endless search for something brighter, bigger, and better. So stop striving and fixing, and start being and exemplifying the true perfection that you are already.

Notice the destination of each moment. Notice the value and the opportunity for joy that exists right now. Each moment and each experience is a destination unto itself. It is only a matter of perception and choice that's keeping you away from experiencing the now, and all the blessings that lie within it. So appreciate the opportunities before you in the present and you will create a series of joyous moments that will make up a happy lifetime.

Now is the time to wake up to where you are and who you are. Now is the time to acknowledge the creation that is happening all around you in each moment. Now is the time to realize that you have already arrived somewhere, and that this somewhere is pretty special.

APPLICATION:

Take a moment to notice, actually notice, in as many moments as you can within this day, how many times you are arriving to something. No matter how small it may seem, find a way to appreciate the place you're in right now because nothing is too small to appreciate. Take the time to appreciate everything that is manifesting for you right now. Notice where you are, what you are doing, and who you are with, knowing that each moment is providing you with something special in its own unique way.

Chapter 19:
Observing the Observer

Change comes from awareness, but awareness comes from observation.

Ever get the feeling that there's more to life than meets the eye? Well there is. The truth is that we are all spiritual and dynamic beings having a physical experience here on earth. We are made of an Infinite Energy that moves beyond space and time and physicality. We are one with the energy that makes up everything and everyone. We are infinite and we are expansive. We are definitely more than meets the eye.

No matter what you have going on in your life, no matter where you are or what you are doing, there is always an Infinite Presence, an Infinite Knowledge that is within you. To access it all you need to do is get present enough to notice it. It is always with you; you just need to awaken to its presence.

At your core you are whole. There is nothing you lack. There is nothing you fear. Your true self knows the truth and the truth is all good. Your higher-self knows the answers to everything you need to know. At your core you are true knowledge and total well-being.

As such, whenever you feel overwhelmed with responsibilities, whenever you feel lost and confused about which path to take next, all you need to do is step away from your judgments and step into a zone of observation.

Through observation you can realize your true values, your false beliefs, and what you genuinely want to express in life. As a result, you will be able to dream big and fulfill your desires from a place of truth and wholeness. Also, when you are in a mode of observation you can recognize your reactions and the nature of your inner chatter, and in doing so, you can become aware of what's actually keeping you from living the life you want to live.

Observing the observer simply means noticing yourself with whatever you are doing, feeling, and thinking. It's like stepping away from your fears, doubts, and worries for long enough to observe them objectively. It's like you are both the one having the experience and the one observing the experience all at the same time.

To explain further, imagine yourself as an actor in a movie. Then imagine watching yourself on the screen of life. You are in the movie and watching the movie all at the same time. What this exercise does is it allows you to become more objective about what you see. You can then see things from a new perspective; not the one where your fears are in control, but the one where you can see what is truly happening, you can objectively assess the situation, and you can make proactive decisions with a clear mind.

Observing yourself and what you are experiencing without judgment allows you to neutralize any resistance you may be feeling in the moment. When this happens, you are then able to freely let go of what you no longer need, shift focus onto the essence of what you would like to experience instead, and feel that essence fully as who you are right now.

Observation is not about dwelling on "what is" and feeling sorry for yourself because of it. It is simply a way for you to release judgment and resistance about what you don't like so that you are free to focus on what you do like.

The point is, rather than getting caught up in what you don't like about your life, you can observe it as it is and learn to appreciate the opportunities that are being presented to you in the moment. Then you can release your resistance, take responsibility, and move on to a better feeling, knowing that you can experience the essence of what you love at any time. Observation allows you to accept "what is," appreciate it as feedback, and then move forward to manifest what you truly love.

Observe things neutrally as they are. Observe the sensations you are feeling objectively rather than trying to fight them off. Observe where you are right now, understand the feedback that this is giving you, and then use that feedback to re-adjust your focus.

Observation is about directing your focus, but it's also about how you perceive the subject of that focus. Meaning, it's not the observation alone that gives meaning to something; it's the perception you choose that creates the meaning for you. So, the point here is to be objective in your observations rather than pre-judging them so that your assessments become more accurate. Then you will be able to transform your observations into something positive through your choice of perception. So release your assumptions, which often come from your fears, doubts, and insecurities anyway, and embrace an open mind and an open heart instead.

The truth is that we judge all the time. It's how we make our decisions in life. We take in the "facts" at hand, we make a judgment or assessment based on what we think we know of in the moment, and then we act on that assessment. However, when we can observe things objectively, we are then able to make more accurate assessments, which then lead us to making more proactive choices. When we can observe in this way, it makes us more aware of guidance and more open to receiving the answers we seek. It reduces our prejudice, and as such, allows us to be more objectively aware of what's truly going on.

Observing ourselves and our reactions in life helps us understand the concept of a bigger picture. When we realize in the moment that we may not yet be aware of all the pieces of the puzzle as they will come together, we are less likely to make hasty judgments about what we deem as being "good" or "bad." We must recognize that sometimes things aren't always as they seem.

It's easy to rush to judgment about what we're experiencing in our lives. But understand that this is the ego's attempt to protect us. We make hasty assumptions simply from our own place of fear and insecurity. But in order to manifest true joy and fulfillment we must be willing to be patient, observant, and open to other possibilities. Judge not by what you see alone, because what you see may just be an illusion.

Having said that, it's important that you are not afraid to make decisions based on the information you have at hand either. While making hasty judgments can lead to faulty interpretations, at some point you're going to have to make some sort of assessment in order to move forward. The key, then, is to be more objective in your assessments so that you are open to seeing the truth rather than just what your ego wants to see.

The bottom line is that the decisions you make next will be based on your assessments that preceded them, so don't just see what you want to see. You don't want to end up ignoring important signs that are telling you to head in another direction. The key is to be open and observant, patient and optimistic, while at the same time knowing when it's time to make a decision based on what you know of in the moment. Let yourself be guided and then move forward on that guidance. Make proactive assessments rather than negative judgments. That way you will know when to hold off, and when to move forward. You have all the information you need at your finger tips. Just let go of your own agendas and fears and allow the truth to come out.

APPLICATION:

The next time you're in a situation where you are feeling reactive, step away from your emotions for one moment and observe yourself in your response. Observe the actual dialogue within your mind as it is happening, and objectively notice the feelings this evokes within you. By doing so you will end up taking the robotic nature out of your reaction, while at the same time placing yourself in a proactive state of mind where your solutions actually reside.

For example, if/when you feel yourself getting reactive in a situation ask yourself, "What am I truly upset about?" "What do I want that I am not getting right now?" The answer to this may or may not come right away, but regardless, take a deep breath and regroup. At the very least you will have taken some sort of step in the right direction. Now, it may be hard to regroup in the heat of the moment, but if you manage it you will realize a solution much faster than if you get caught up in anger or frustration. By all means, feel what you feel, just don't get lost in it.

When you get into a place of objective observation you will realize that what you want goes a lot deeper than what's appearing on the surface. For instance, your rage about your spouse leaving an empty milk carton in the fridge may really be coming from a desire to feel respected and appreciated. Or your anger towards someone who is taking you for granted may really be anger at yourself for allowing this to happen, which is really an expression of your desire to respect yourself more. Your awareness, then, can actually help you release your anger and hurt a lot faster because it will help you realize that your reaction is simply a cover-up for how you truly feel and what you truly want. And by understanding your true feelings you will be better able to ask for what you truly desire rather than getting caught up in your ego's reactions.

Observation brings awareness into the present moment, and with awareness comes consciousness. Through consciousness you can then shift into making more proactive choices. As you become more conscious of what's going on, you'll see more clearly the errors in your thinking, as well as the false beliefs you've adopted that caused you to react in the first place.

If you are unhappy with something in your life, don't fight against it. Observe it, take responsibility for it, know that you can change it, and just let it be for right now. Know that as you release your resistance to it and as you release your false beliefs about it, you will be able to move on to something more fulfilling that much sooner.

If faced with a circumstance that you don't particularly like, observe it without judgment; be neutral. Approach it with an attitude of, "Hmm, this is interesting," rather than placing a negative judgment on it right away. Because when you are neutral in this way it creates an opening for you to focus on what you do want because you are no longer focusing on what you don't want.

Observing yourself from an objective standpoint can have many benefits. Not only can it help you more accurately assess the situation at hand, it can also lead you to make more proactive choices. Whether you are feeling anxious or delighted, observing yourself will help you realize the truth of your feelings, where they are coming from, and if need be, how to transform them into ones that will do you the most justice.

Understand that observation is not just about observing your negative reactions and feelings. In fact, it's just as important, if not more so, to notice what feels authentically good to you. So notice those experiences with which you feel joy and fulfillment because these represent your true nature. Notice yourself having these experiences. Feel the proactive gratitude for their expression in your life and for the fact that they are showing you how aligned you truly are. Observe how you feel. Register these moments in your memory bank and recall them whenever you need a reminder of the joyous and blessed person you truly are.

Know that observation can also help you develop your intuition. By being aware of your body, your feelings, your thoughts, and the overall sensations you are experiencing in any given moment, you will better recognize when your intuition is talking to you. For instance, pay particular attention to how you are feeling right before you ask for guidance. This way you will be able to notice a shift in energy, physical sensation, feeling, and/or thought process as it happens. And when you do notice a shift, you will know how your higher-self speaks to you, and you will know the difference between your ego's voice and the voice of Divine Guidance.

Finally, observing yourself can help you recognize and release any subconscious beliefs that may be stopping you from manifesting what you desire most. Understand that if your conscious mind and your subconscious mind are not aligned, you will feel resistance either within yourself or mirrored in the outside world as your life experience. So how do you know if you are resisting your desire? Well, by observing how you feel about it.

Start by envisioning your desire. How does it feel to be, do, and/or have it? As you are envisioning and feeling this desire, ask yourself, "Do I believe I can manifest this?" "What is my belief about my ability to have this?" If any feelings or excuses that indicate a "no" come up, you know that your subconscious mind is not aligned with your intention, and therefore, every time you think about, affirm, or envision your desire you are holding resistance to it, which is likely preventing it from manifesting.

When you are able to observe how you truly feel in the moment about what you want, you become acutely aware of where you may be blocking yourself from receiving it. If you are not observant of this, then you could end up with wonderful fantasies that never end up manifesting. So instead of just visualizing a desired outcome, understand how you feel about the possibility of this outcome. And instead of feeling doubtful, feel that this outcome is in some way possible for you, or at the very least, don't be resistant to it. As long as you think of it as a possibility, no matter how remote, you will be leaving an opening for it. Simply envision it for the fun of it, because as long as you are not dwelling in persistent doubt, even if you don't completely believe it will manifest, at least you will be energetically open to it and not resisting it. Regardless, if you aren't observant with yourself you will not know how you truly feel about anything.

For example, say your desire is to travel more. Start out by envisioning a scenario where you see yourself traveling and enjoying yourself. Feel how good it feels to imagine this outcome. Now ask yourself whether or not you believe this is possible for you. Notice if any excuses come up like, "I can't afford it," "I haven't been able to do it so far," "I don't have the time," "I don't deserve it," etc.

Notice if your negative perceptions and persistent doubts have been affecting what you believe about your future. Also notice any subconscious beliefs that may be stifling the manifestation of your desires, and know that without observation you will not likely know what those are. Observation, then, allows you to uncover your true beliefs and transform them where needed so that your conscious intentions align with your subconscious beliefs.

In order to change your circumstances you must change your habits and patterns of belief. But you cannot know what you truly believe if you do not observe yourself long enough to notice. Your subconscious mind is based on habits and patterns of thought, so no matter what your conscious mind is doing, if your subconscious is not aligned with your intentions, it will likely be more difficult to attain the results you seek. So observe yourself and your thoughts and feelings in the present so that you can truthfully know what your subconscious mind is thinking, as well as how you're truly feeling about your intentions.

Know that you can direct your subconscious mind more easily when you are present and aware of what's going on within you and around you at any given moment. Then through your awareness you can choose the programming you want so that what you desire most is what naturally manifests in your life rather than repressed fears, doubts, and faulty beliefs.

Understand that if you do not question yourself about what you truly believe, you will be allowing your negative auto-pilot to control your life. But if you do stop yourself in the moment and question how you truly feel about yourself, what you want, and your worthiness of having it, then you will notice patterns of negative thinking that you need to change. In this way you will no longer be holding resistance to your desires, and as such, you will be able to manifest what you love that much easier.

Chapter 20:
Simplifying

Everything is quite simple when you cease to complicate it.

Simplification is not necessarily about giving up all of your possessions and moving to some remote island or mountain top somewhere to meditate all day long. Simplification is a state of mind, and as such, it can be applied to your consciousness just as much as it can to your physical environment.

Simplification simply means letting go of all the baggage that has been keeping you stuck thus far. Simplification is about removing the clutter from your life, be it mental, emotional, and/or physical. But it's not necessarily about giving up your material things; it's about giving up your attachment to those things.

Some believe that to be truly happy they must simplify their lives by giving up their material possessions. Now, if that's something that resonates with you, then that's fine, but know that it's not necessary to do in order to achieve simplicity and happiness in your life. Simplification starts in your consciousness. Some may need to physically clear things out in order to mentally and emotionally clear things out, and that's ok. But that's a personal choice. Know that you can learn to simplify your life simply by redefining the meaning you place on the material rather than getting rid of it altogether.

Being happy is a choice, no matter what you physically have or don't have. And simplifying your life is truly a matter of being clear about your consciousness. You can have a lot and feel poor, and you can have a little and feel rich. It's all a matter of perception. Simplification starts in the mind and carries over into your physical affairs accordingly. If you feel spiritually full, then whether you have a little or a lot, materially speaking, you already know you have it all.

Simplification is about clearing confusion. It's about asking questions and receiving answers. It's about letting go of the struggle, thereby allowing yourself to be guided in the direction of your purpose and total fulfillment. It's about living in the moment.

Some say ignorance is bliss, but it's not so blissful when you can't understand why you keep attracting the same patterns over and over. Being ignorant does not simplify your life at all. In fact, ignorance ultimately leads to confusion and frustration. Knowledge and awareness, on the other hand, allow you to understand more, and therefore, to adjust your thinking in such a way that releases the struggle, and subsequently, simplifies your life.

Simplification comes of presence. When you are present and aware you are more open to receiving the guidance and knowledge you need to live a joyous life. You are able to clarify your understanding of the world, and subsequently, push confusion to the wayside. You are able to learn more, grow more, expand more, and create for yourself a more dynamic, knowledgeable, creative, and peaceful existence. In your awareness you will find the simple truth that's been with you all along.

When you are aware of and knowledgeable about yourself, life, and The Universe as a whole, you are better equipped to let go and allow what's best for you to unfold. The laws of The Universe are actually a lot simpler than you might think. Understand that you don't have to know how these laws work, or even that they exist, in order for them to work for you. In fact, they are at work all the time. But by being aware of them it will help take the randomness out of your life and help you release your victim mentality, thereby bringing you into self-empowerment. You will be able to participate in the creation of your own life experiences with presence and intention. By understanding the workings of The Universe you will be able to surrender to it and allow your good to flow to you without obstruction.

Simplification is about understanding the order of things, or at least acknowledging that there is one. When you see things as random it ends up creating more stress and complication in your life because you see your future as uncertain, unstable, and beyond your control. However, when you believe in order and co-creation, you are then able to let go into the flow of life with trust and patience. The unknown no longer scares you, and as a result, you are able to live in peace and harmony.

Seeing the world as random brings more confusion and chaos into your life. It causes you to feel hopeless and disempowered. But when you become aware of the synchronicities in your life, i.e. those events that you just can't pass off as coincidences, you become more at peace and more centered. You start to see the order within the chaos. And when you become conscious to this order you will realize how empowered you really are; you will realize that there is an Energy Source that is behind everything, and that you are one with this Source too.

Don't see things as randomly happening to you. Understand the cause and effect relationship. Then you will also understand the power you hold to shape your own life. You put out a certain vibe into the world, and eventually if you don't change it, that vibe will come back to you in a seemingly random set of events and circumstances that really aren't random at all. You may not see the connection so you may decide it's just good luck or bad luck that comes from "out of the blue," but in reality it's all connected. Just because you don't yet understand the connection between events doesn't mean it's not there. So be more aware and you will start to notice the synchronicities around you, which will simplify your perspective on life. Everything does have its reason so trust in that, whether things go the way you want them to or not.

Simplification is about understanding the world around you and the cause and effect relationship. When we see things as occurring randomly, the world can come off as unfair and unjust. When selfless people appear to be "wronged" we don't understand why. When seemingly innocent people are born into hard circumstances, we question the Powers That Be.

But this is a practical issue as much as it is a philosophical one. When we deem something as being unfair or unjust it's because we don't fully grasp the full picture. There is an order that underlies everything, and when you still yourself for just a moment you will begin to see and feel the connection.

You must understand that the law of cause and effect is not lost on anyone, just like the law of gravity. Whether you believe in it or not it still applies to you. When you understand this, while you may not agree with them, the injustices of the world suddenly start to make a bit more sense. While outer appearances may show one thing, in actuality, the life path, personal journey, thoughts, beliefs, feelings, actions, unique purpose, karma (which is really the law of cause and effect at work), and concept of self-worth of any individual are what generally cause them to attract to themselves their life's circumstances. But without fail, no what matter their circumstances, they can always make conscious choices that can bring about change.

You too have come here with a purpose. You too have choices. You can choose to see your life as random and chaotic, or you can choose to use the feedback you get to make positive choices in each moment. You can choose to see yourself as the cause in your life rather than just the effect of a random world. Then you will be empowered to create, and then your life will feel simplified.

Simplifying is truly about letting go. When you are able to let go of your worries, your fears, and your need to know in advance how everything will come together, you will find yourself feeling more at peace and more aligned with the joyous flow of life.

Simplifying is about focusing on the moment at hand. As you do, your life will become simpler and easier to manage. You will no longer feel overwhelmed because everything will feel clear to you. As you focus on one moment at a time you will be allowing things to unfold naturally and with ease. You will be able to appreciate the moment and trust that everything is working out for the best.

Simplification is also about setting priorities. When you are scattered and confused about what to do you may end up taking on too much at once. Conversely, when you prioritize and organize what you need to do in order of importance to you, you'll end up finding more efficient and more effective ways of getting things done. The better you know your priorities, the easier it will be for you to decide on your actions, and when you feel confident in your actions, you bring simplification, order, and peace back into your life.

Simplifying your life is really about understanding the power of the present moment. When you are aware of the present moment your thoughts are not on what you need to do next or what you "should have" done earlier. Your focus is simply on the task at hand, which makes things a lot simpler. As you move from step to step in this manner, and treat each moment as its own goal, the path to your fulfillment becomes that much simpler and more enjoyable.

Simplification is really about appreciating and enjoying each moment. When you can appreciate each step along your path you will no longer feel the need to obsess over what you want for tomorrow. As a result, you will feel more content and trusting, which will ultimately bring more peace and joy into your life.

Right now is what you have, and right now isn't as complicated as you might think, no matter how it may seem. Even as you ponder your future you can do so from a place of peace and joy, feeling the essence of what you love right now, and knowing that reaching your goals is a lot simpler than you might think. All you need to do is align with your true self and all the complications and stress will melt away. Bring it all back to the basics by being authentic and honest with yourself and others. Then you can focus on each moment, and step by step, you will reach your goals with fun, joy, ease, and simplicity.

APPLICATION:

Think of an area that causes you stress. Where in your life do you feel overwhelmed? Once you've come up with your answer, list all the things that are worrying you in relation to that area of your life right now.

If you break down your worries you will notice how many of them are real threats, how many of them are hypothetical, how many of them are based on negative perceptions and fears, and how many of them, if any, actually exist right now.

Now go through your list and organize your worries into "Things that are within my control right now" and "Things that I have no idea what to do with right now." With those things you know how to handle, prioritize them into mini-goals or tasks and then choose the first on your list and focus only on doing that. Be present with it. Find the joy and blessing in it. See it as an opportunity to do something great. Leave all the other stuff until you are ready to address it. Remember, this is something you have prioritized and chosen to do.

For those things on your "Things that I have no idea what to do with right now" list, let them go. Decide on the essence that you are looking to feel, and then focus your attention only on that right now. For example, this could be joy, peace, clarity, success, etc. Trust that as you come closer to doing these things, a way will show up and you will know what to do. For now, there is no sense in worrying about it. Just take one step at a time and do what you know to do in the moment. This will not only automatically simplify and de-stress your life, it will also help you get clarity on what to do next. Take your mind off your worries. Focus on something else for the moment, and by doing so you will free your mind to receive the solutions you seek.

Declare that everything goes smoothly for you and that you always know exactly what to do in each moment. Doing this will release your worries and bring peace and order back into the moment. The key to remember is patience. The more patient you are, the less stressed you'll feel, and the faster you'll get the answers you seek.

Take some time to de-clutter your physical environment too. You do not need to be a neat-freak all the time. Just keep your environment relatively clean and free of clutter and this will keep you clear and receptive as well. When your environment is cluttered it has an effect on your psyche. It can also cause stagnation from an energetic point of view. Clearing clutter will clear your space so that energy can flow freely.

Physical de-cluttering is a great catalyst for emotional and mental de-cluttering too. This doesn't mean you need to give it all away. Just clear out those things you no longer use or need. As you let go of those things you no longer need, you will free yourself of stagnated energy, which will then unblock your flow of good.

Simplification is about clarity and getting to the core, to the root, to the basics of that which runs your life. Don't complicate your life more than is necessary. Check in with yourself from time to time and ask yourself if things are really as complicated as you think they are. Chances are they are not. Get to the root of what you want to express in your life. Be honest about your motives. Look to see what's right there in front of you, for the answers you seek are already within you, waiting for you to take notice. Be present in your life and you will see how simple and joyous your life can really be. Remember, simplification is not about sacrifice or deprivation. It's about realizing how blessed you really are, right now and always.

Finally, take the time to learn about the laws of The Universe as this will help you better understand your own power, and subsequently, help you simplify your life. Strike up a healthy balance between learning and applying, absorbing and processing, and do it all at your own pace. Learn the fundamentals and build your knowledge from there. That way no matter how much there is to learn and no matter how many questions you have unanswered, you will always feel simplified in your approach, and you will always be able to handle the information that's given to you.

Chapter 21:
Planning for the Future

Plan ahead, just don't lose your head.

With all this talk about presence and living in the moment, one question remains looming: where does planning fit in? If you are focusing only on the moment at hand, how can you simultaneously plan for the future?

Well, to start, understand that being present is really about seeing the moment at hand as an opportunity to shape your reality. It's about being conscious of your thoughts, feelings, beliefs, and actions in the moment so that you can make choices out of that consciousness. It's about being able to make plans for future events, set goals, and create timelines, all the while being mindful of the present moment.

When you are mindful you are able to plan your future from a place of wholeness, trust, and surrender. You can sketch out what you would like to occur, while at the same time being aware of the guidance you are receiving in each of your present moments. You can think about future events, but at the same time, feel them in the present, and then use those feelings to guide you to your best decisions.

Planning is future-focused. But right here and right now is the time in which ideas are being born. Right here and right now is where the power to shape your life resides. Your past, your present, your future, they're all one right now within your consciousness, and you get to choose where your focus goes. All you need to do is be aware of the present moment and allow your consciousness to focus on what you truly love. Envision yourself already being who you desire to be. Feel yourself in the reality of your choosing right now.

Living in the moment does not mean that you can never plan for your future. In fact, you are planning for your future in each of your present moments. Every thought, every feeling, every action is bringing you your personal reality. Your "right now" is creating your tomorrow.

No matter what you are thinking about, whether it's the past, present, or future, your thoughts are really happening in the now. So when you plan for your future, just stay aware of the moment at hand rather than getting too ahead of yourself. Meaning, don't get lost in trying to figure out all the details ahead of time. There are certainly some things you can plan for and predict, but there are also some things that are simply unknown to you at this time, i.e. there are plenty of pleasant surprises awaiting you but you don't need to figure them all out in advance.

So plan what you need to plan, but also be open to other possibilities; possibilities that may in fact be even better than what you had imagined. Plan your future with the present in mind. Feel your future as something tangible in your mind's eye now. Then, be aware of the guidance you're receiving now, and use that guidance to make your decisions for what you plan on doing next. Go ahead, plan ahead, just don't lose sight of the only moment that ever truly exists, and that's now.

Timelines:

What inspires us to set timelines in the first place? Well for one, we fear the unknown, and because of that we allow our ego to dictate when and how things "should" happen based on our incessant desire for instant gratification. Now, this isn't always the case, but in too many instances it is.

Consequently, setting timelines can sometimes send a needy message to The Universe. It's like saying, "Hey Universe, I really need this to happen by such and such date in order for me to be happy." But neediness is a symptom of a lack consciousness, and through lack you'll only attract more lack, and that's counter-productive.

Setting a due date hoping that by doing so you will hurry the process along may cause you to become desperate and attached to the outcome of

Planning for the Future

your goal, and as we know, attachment is a buzz-kill for the manifestation process. Trying to force or rush the process in order to feel happier than you are right now will ultimately cause you more stress and struggle.

But what if you could find the contentment you seek within you right now? What if your happiness didn't depend on some goal manifesting two months from now or one week from now, or whenever? Then you could focus on the essence of happiness right now, thereby allowing yourself to go with the flow, which would then allow your goals to manifest naturally and without pressure.

Having said all that, setting timelines can be beneficial too, but only if they are set with the right intention. For example, where timelines can be helpful is when they work as motivators. Sometimes we procrastinate. Sometimes we allow our fears, and subsequent excuses, to stop us from taking action. In those instances we are allowing our insecurities to run our lives. If/when this happens, setting a timeline for yourself can be helpful for getting you organized and moving forward on your goals.

Timelines can also help you focus on and choose activities that are aligned with your goals rather than those that sidetrack you if/when your doubts and fears resurface. The key, however, is to let go of your attachment to any specific timing because this can cause delay in your manifestation process. Simply set the timeline, do your best to keep it, use it to motivate you and keep you on track, but also stay flexible and open to guidance, as well as any shifts that may be necessary along the way. Don't be so strict that you close yourself off from inspiration and spontaneity. Be determined but be flexible too. Add, "This, or something better" to your intentions and timelines so that while you are free to move forward on them, you are still open to other possibilities if they are better than the ones you've laid out for yourself.

You'll really only know if something is right for you if you are willing to let go of your attachment to it. You can certainly push something to occur in your life, but it may be less than what you can actually have. If you let go of your need to control every detail, however, then you can trust that as you align with your true self, everything you manifest, and the time in which it manifests, will be perfect for you.

As a general rule, decide to do everything you know of on a daily basis that is aligned with your truth. That way you won't be fixated on timelines because you will already be motivated and acting on your goals in each moment, whether it's in thought, feeling, attitude, action, or all the above. This will leave room for guidance and inspiration to come to you, moment by moment. You'll essentially be allowing your joy to manifest in the best ways, naturally and joyously. You don't have to know when and how. Just go about your business and trust that everything is unfolding in the perfect way.

Rushing the process indicates fear, lack, and impatience. And there's a big difference between rushing your goal and moving towards it. It's one thing to use a timeline as a motivator with the purpose of inspiring yourself to reach and even surpass your potential. It's another thing to use a timeline as a means for pressuring yourself and your goal to manifest sooner because you feel a lack of it in your life right now.

Understand that you do not really lack anything. If you take on the attitude of being whole, then you will manifest that which is aligned with that wholeness. Know that you can be happy now and move forward in expressing that happiness in every moment. You can be content with what you have, and express and manifest more of that contentment at the same time. Simply appreciate your "right now," while feeling already connected to what's to come. It's as simple as that.

Manifestation takes all sorts of elements into consideration. It's not just about getting what you want when you want it. It also involves other factors that need to come into alignment with each other; and there is an infinite amount of possible elements and variations. But if those other elements are not yet aligned, setting overly specific timelines may get you some variation of what you are looking to receive, but it may not be the best variation for you. If you are patient, however, and leave the timetable up to The Universe,

Planning for the Future

what is best for you will show up in the time and order that is right for you. So instead of settling for less out of impatience, you will get that which is most aligned with your ultimate fulfillment.

Don't let timelines trick you into thinking that you need something to happen in order for you to be happy. Often times when we set timelines for ourselves it's out of a feeling of lack. We want something to occur because we believe it will make us happier than we are right now. So we try to place pressure on ourselves and on The Universe to deliver what we want sooner rather than later because we feel we need that thing, person, and/or experience in order to feel happy and whole. But this is not the truth. You can feel whole and happy as you are right now. You can leave the timing to The Universe and approach your goals with a sense of wonder, excitement, and trust. Yes, you can set timelines, but let these timelines serve only as guidelines for you on the action steps you know to take now, rather than as the means to pressure your goals into manifesting.

Ego can cause you to be impatient and unappreciative of what you have now. It can cause you to lose sight of the journey itself and it can create a very future-focused reality for you in which the outcome becomes your main and only goal. But do not allow yourself to get lost in future projections at the expense of the present moment. Give yourself permission to freely flow down your path, enjoying and admiring, appreciating and experiencing all the moments along the way.

Who's to say for sure that the due date you've chosen is the best one for you anyway? How did you come to setting this date in the first place? Was it ego-driven or soul-inspired? At the end of the day, know that an inner calling would never leave you feeling desperate or fearful. It would inspire you to take joyous action in the present moment with a vision of what can come, but without the need to define it or push it into existence. Remember this as you move forward in the creation of your life.

Specifics:

Outlining the specifics of your future can get a little tricky. This is because often when we think of specifics we also get quite attached to them, which leaves us very closed-off to guidance and inspiration. So instead, we must use specifics mindfully, rather than desperately, in order to get us fully into the present moment and manifesting the best results.

Understand that underneath anything and everything that you desire lies an essence. Because of this, you can access the essence of anything you desire at any time, including right now. So if underneath all the specifics the essence is what you seek, then why not start with experiencing that essence now? Why not align with your truth and allow the specifics to be inspired by your core? Then you will be able to go about your day, moment by moment, all the while feeling happy and fulfilled, and trusting that the specifics you need to know about will come to you when the time is right. And when they do, you will be able to confidently take inspired action on them and then let go into the process all over again.

In truth, the best use for specifics is to help you get into the essence feeling of what you love. And when you focus on the essence of your desires, as opposed to specifics alone, you leave room for guidance and flexibility. You leave room for your purpose to inspire you, and when it does, you can confidently act on those specifics right in the moment without hesitation.

You don't need to worry over specifics. In fact, it's when you get too attached to them that you move away from the natural flow of your life. And it's when you get too attached and start to control everything that you start feeling stressed. However, when you focus your attention on the essence you love and feel that experience in your present moments, that's when you become empowered and inspired. That's when the specifics show up to guide you along your purposeful path.

Understand that The Universe is totally impartial. It will bring you whatever you are in alignment with. So it would make sense that you focus your attention on feeling good now, and feeling the essence of what you love now. You can certainly use specifics to help you cultivate those feelings of alignment, but then let go of them. Then you will be using specifics to your advantage rather than having them hamper your progress.

Specific focus can be very helpful in painting for you a picture of what you desire to express the most. It can help you narrow your focus enough to fully believe in and act upon that which you want to manifest. It can help ground you in the present moment by helping you cultivate the essence feeling of what you truly love. And it can be helpful in directing your focus away from doubt and towards faith instead. Just don't get too attached.

For example, say you intend to manifest a million dollars. You can figure out the logistics to help your rational mind believe in this possibility. You can think of various ways this can happen and brainstorm ideas. For instance, you may decide that one way could be to sell your product or service, in which case you could calculate how many units or hours you would need to sell in order to make that million. But you don't have to know how everything will come together right now. You don't have to figure it all out in advance. You can work out some of the potential specifics so that your rational mind does not contradict or resist your intention, but then you can let it all go.

While you can certainly focus on specifics and logistics, remember that you're not in this alone. So let go of your agendas and attachments and let yourself go into Divine Guidance and Flow. Embrace the attitude of allowing, "This, or something better" to manifest, and you will be relaxed and in the flow of life in each moment.

Keep in mind that specific focus is not for the benefit of The Universe to know what you want, because The Universe is all-knowing. Specific focus is for your benefit. It's so that you can align with your truth beyond any doubt. It's so that you can surrender yourself to infinite joyous possibilities. It's so that you can allow yourself to dream big without being hindered by limitations.

Understand that we live in an environment that often compartmentalizes what we can and cannot be, do, and have. As a result, if we're not diligent with our focus, we may end up falling victim to the collective beliefs that may or may not be good for us. Being specific in your focus, then, can help you align with what you truly love and desire to manifest by helping you direct your energy in a positive way. It can help you align with your core and your purpose beyond any collective doubts or societal pressures. It can keep you motivated and moving towards fulfilling your purpose. However, where it gets counter-productive is when you allow yourself to get too attached to the specifics you've laid out for yourself.

If you get too attached to specifics you may end up following the whims of your ego versus the inspirations of your soul. As a result, you may end up with those specifics, but they may not lead you to the ultimate happiness and fulfillment you seek.

But by being present and aware in the moment you become conscious of the drive behind your intentions, and as such, you become better able to determine if your intentions are purpose-driven or inspired by ego. And when you know the difference, you are then able to focus naturally on the specifics that are most authentic to you.

The key to remember is alignment. And certainly one way to stay aligned is to direct your focus with specifics. The key, though, is to do it with detachment and surrender. The key is to use these specifics as a means for aligning rather than a means for manifesting. Then you will have the best of both worlds, the specifics that drive you, and the surrender that allows things to happen.

Remember, The Universe already knows what you want. Right now you have every bit of your potential within you, and The Universe knows what that is. Keep in mind that you are "asking" through your vibration and that The Universe is yielding to that vibration. Know too that your ultimate drive is your purpose, and purpose is something that is always with you; it's what ultimately inspires you, and as long as you're aligned with it, it's what The Universe responds to as well. So don't worry about whether or not The Universe hears you or knows the specifics of what you want. Rather, stay adequately aligned with your core, your authenticity, and the essence of what you love, and The Universe will deliver.

Trust that as you align with your true self, the specifics will come. Sure, have your ideas, and even act on them, but also let go and allow for flexibility. Know that specifics have their place in the manifestation process, but they needn't be something you rely on completely. You have to learn to be patient and trust in Universal Timing and Order. You need to not settle for less than you deserve and love out of impatience or haste, because you truly can have the best.

Being patient and trusting in Divine Timing doesn't mean you stop taking proactive action. You can still take action towards your goals; just stop dictating all the conditions before hand. Remember that forcing specific outcomes is a desire of the ego. Your higher-self already knows the perfect timing and order for everything. All you need to do is not resist it. As long as you are aligned with your authenticity, you won't have to worry about specifics. And when they do inspire you, you will be able to act on them and detach from them just the same.

So if you choose to outline and focus on a specific goal, do it for the sake of aligning in the moment with the feeling of it, and to keep your thoughts, feelings, beliefs, and actions aligned with that feeling as well. Do it for the sake of your own clarity and focus. Then take inspired action, let go of your attachments to the outcome, and just allow the rest to unfold naturally. Trust in the guidance you receive and take it one step at a time. Trust that each step is taking you in the right direction, and then simply enjoy the journey along the way.

Measurable Goals:

What about measurable goals? We are often told to create measurable goals so that we know when we have achieved them. While this can certainly be an effective tool, in the bigger picture, the real measuring stick needs to be how you feel. Everything you want in life has to do with the feeling and the experience you are looking to receive from it. So the real measure of your goals needs to be how you feel about them right now.

For example, say your goal is to make an extra $ (whatever the amount) a month. That seems like a measurable goal in that you will know when you've reached it. However, going deeper, you need to ask yourself what this extra money represents to you. What's the essence of it? What do you really want underneath it all? Is it a sense of accomplishment and self-esteem, a feeling of security and success? Once you've realized the real measure of your goal, i.e. the essence of it, you can then work on cultivating that feeling right in the now.

For instance, you can choose to feel secure by knowing that you are one with the Source of All There Is, and that this Source is your ultimate provider. You can feel good about yourself because you know you are infinite in your potential and bound by nothing, and that true success is measured by the person you are rather than just by what you have. You can choose to appreciate the wealth in your life right now and grow your wealth from there as an expression of your truth. You can also realize that your potential needn't be limited by any specifics you've laid out for yourself and that if you let go a little, you can manifest even more than what you thought was possible for you simply by tapping into the truth of your limitless potential. These are the real measures you need to be looking out for.

So go ahead and create measurable goals, just be sure to also feel the essence of what you love right now and let that be the measuring stick you use to gauge your level of success in each moment. Learn to let go of any attachments you have to the outcome of things as well. That way you will simply be focused on the essence of what you love. Then as you align with this essence, it will start to show itself in your external environment too with ease and joy.

APPLICATION:

The next time you are planning something, take a moment to understand the essence of what you are hoping to receive from it. For example, say you are planning your next vacation, before you delve into the logistics of your planning, think about how experiencing this vacation might feel to you. Will you feel calm, rejuvenated, relaxed, invigorated, stimulated, excited, etc?

Next, once you have established your present focus, continue to move forward with your planning activities, all the while realizing that the way you feel about your plans right now is actually contributing to the experiences you are drawing forth to yourself. While you are planning, do your best to stay mindful of how you are feeling about your plans in the present moment. Be aware that the energy you are cultivating around your plans is the energy that will be attracted back to you. So leave your worries and doubts out of it and focus only on the joy you feel and anticipate.

Also, be present in your planning activity. Use it as an exercise in awareness by really being open to guidance every step of the way. This way even as you plan, you will still be aware of the present moment and the information you are being given in that moment. It is when you can hone your ability to be present and aware, even in the midst of planning for the future, that you are able to make your best choices.

Yes, planning is a future-focused activity, and we do sometimes need to plan out what we want to do, be, and have. So the point is not to eliminate planning, but rather to localize it within your consciousness so that even when you are thinking about the future, you are able to experience what you desire right now in your mind and in your heart.

If you become aware of your feelings right now you will realize the types of experiences you are drawing forth to yourself, and subsequently, you'll be able to actively tweak your thoughts so that they align with what you actually want to manifest.

And if you really feel compelled to set a due date for your goals, or to outline specifics and measures, do it from the perspective of helping yourself focus rather than attaching yourself to any one outcome. Let your focus fall first and foremost on your alignment with your authentic self, and as you do, your goals, timelines, specifics, plans, desires, ideas, and actions will all naturally flow to you in each moment.

Chapter 22:

Being in the Flow and Fulfilling Your Desires

The stream knows the way to the ocean.

Contrary to popular belief, struggle is not natural to life. It may appear as such, but it's simply a misconception. Struggle comes of misaligned thinking, and whether you were born into struggle or not, its maintenance in your life is simply the result of your perpetually present negative beliefs and attitudes. It's simply the result of the stories you keep telling yourself and others about how you are a victim of circumstance. But understand that the stronger your beliefs, the more likely they will become your truths. So if you want to shift your life around for the better, you must start from the inside and get into the flow of the person you truly are rather than the one you've been told you are, or the one you've falsely labeled yourself to be.

In order to be in the flow of life, and benefit from it, you must be willing to release the beliefs that no longer serve you. Unfortunately, negative beliefs are often hidden behind the guise of normalcy and pragmatism in our world, and as such, we end up taking them on as our natural state of being. Negative beliefs are truly the security blanket of society, and have been since the dawn of civilization.

Beliefs like, "Nothing comes easy," "Money doesn't grow on trees," and implications that we need to be "realistic" have instilled in us a very pessimistic outlook on life. However, just because these beliefs have been passed down to us through generations of popular opinion, it doesn't mean we need to adopt them as our own. We can be trend-setters and leaders in our own right. We can take solace in the fact that while there have always been those who've said it can't be done, equally, there have always been those who've ended up doing it anyway.

What we really need is a movement of independent thinking where we follow our hearts rather than common or popular opinion alone. What we need is to willingly release the struggle by simply choosing to do so, right here and right now. What we need is to say, "Yes," no matter what others think is or isn't possible.

Subsequently, it is when we are present that we are confidently able to say, "Yes" because we are no longer allowing anything from our past to hold us back, and our future is yet a blank canvas awaiting our creative input. Presence allows us to release the struggle, align with infinite possibilities, and live in the natural flow of life, which has everything to do with the fulfillment of what we truly desire.

Fulfillment is your birthright. All you need to do is recognize and align with this fact. You don't need to earn it; you simply need to accept it, be it, and you will have it to enjoy and share. Earning fulfillment can sometimes feel like a dogmatic practice that comes out of fear and self-righteousness. But true fulfillment is not something you are deprived of or rewarded with. It is something you choose and already have within you.

The concept of earning may indeed be an outdated notion. Perhaps it's time for us to step away from believing that we need to earn our good, and instead, step into a belief that our good is already here and waiting for us to wake up to it. And we wake up to it by being our best selves, by loving our true selves, and by loving and respecting others as well.

Know that you have it in you to be, do, and have in essence anything you desire. All you really need is to get into the flow and allow your desires to be naturally fulfilled in infinitely joyous ways. All you need to do is transform your beliefs, and subsequent behaviors, so that they match the Universal Truths of Infinite Supply and Unconditional Love.

Being in the Flow and Fulfilling Your Desires

In order to naturally fulfill your desires you must feel fulfilled from the inside. You must release your notion of punishment and reward and understand that you are the one that decides the nature of your fate, i.e. the tone of your life experiences. But in order to be a creative partner in your own life you must truly understand the nature of your desires and where your happiness really comes from. You must understand the nature of your partnership with The Universe, do what's yours to do, and leave the rest to something bigger. Your fate and your happiness are essentially in your hands. You can either follow the purposeful guidance you receive, or give in to the whims of your ego; it's your choice.

Being in the flow and fulfilling your desires is about understanding the nature of your desires first and foremost. Where are they coming from? How do you feel about them in the moment? Are they based in feelings of lack, or are they based in wholeness and truth? Know that authentic desires are those that inspire you to express the totality of your potential because you know this potential is already yours. Focus on those desires and you will naturally be aligned with your purpose and your ultimate happiness and success.

The key to happiness is in eliminating a lack mentality and the subsequent desperation that ensues. The key to happiness is in expressing an inner truth rather than trying to fill a perceived void through external means. So ask yourself, "What type of desire am I having right now?" "Is it a type of desire that's causing a longing, craving, or a sense of lack within me?" If so, know that it will only perpetuate the very conditions you want to change. But if it's the type of desire that expresses something you already know to be true in your heart, then it will actually manifest as the change you seek.

Look at your authentic desires as guidance to what's already yours. Then you will be in the flow and ready to receive that which you love. Your authentic desires have reason; they are yours to be fulfilled. Do not suppress them, but do not chase after them either. Have faith in them and use them as your guides. Then let go of them and allow The Universe to deliver what's needed for their fulfillment.

Being in the flow means trusting in a Divine Order, and as such, releasing the struggle that comes from striving to get what you want. It means aligning with your truth and allowing what's best to unfold. It's about trusting that ultimately what you authentically want for yourself is what is also aligned with your true purpose. Your purpose is driving your truest desires, so have faith in the process and let go into the flow, moment by moment, all the way to the manifestation of those desires in your life.

Being in the flow is about having faith, trust, and patience in every moment no matter what your outer conditions may be showing you. Chasing, pushing, forcing, manipulating, or striving will only make you feel more desperate, attached, and insecure. But if you allow yourself to ride the wave of guidance you are being given in every moment, you will fulfill your best desires in the best ways. Know that your job isn't to "make" anything happen. Your job is to allow it to happen, to allow yourself to receive what's truly yours, and then to share your joy with the world.

So instead of chasing after the illusion of happiness, and instead of trying to force things into existence, opt for feeling happy right now. Opt for feeling the essence you desire right now. Opt for appreciating where you are and what you have right now. Feel the perfection within you right now. Trust that all is manifesting in perfect order. Trust that as you let go into the flow of life you will always know what you need to do.

There is no need to rush the process either. Life is not a race or a competition. Understandably your ego wants what it wants immediately, but sometimes what is best needs to wait until you are ready to receive it, i.e. until all the pieces have come together in a way that benefits you and all concerned.

Being in the flow of life is about having an inherent patience that comes out of trust and faith and a knowing that you are already whole and complete as you stand. From this standpoint you will then be in the perfect position to receive all the blessings you have coming to you.

The only real thing standing in the way of you and your authentic desires is your belief in lack. Lack stimulates feelings of desperation, depression, impatience, and all those other ego emotions that cause you stress and struggle. Lack causes you to swim upstream and against the current of life. So drop your own self-imposed limits and learn to trust the process of life; then you will be in the flow. Don't get stuck on your ego's timeline. Let life show you the way, moment by moment, step by step.

Know that you are already one with all that you desire right now. You are so by the very virtue of your being. You are energy, as is everything else. As such, at your core you are connected to everything and everyone. Remember this the next time you feel lack. Your lack is only a perception. The more you choose to feel abundant in each moment, the more abundant you will truly be.

Know that everything you desire is already a possibility. It's here to inspire you, and it expands with your every thought. It's in your consciousness, and as such, it's in the Universal Consciousness. You simply need to align with it to draw its expression forth into your life. Just believe, allow, and relax into the flow.

Understand too that being in the flow and fulfilling your desires is largely dependent upon your ability to be present and aware of your internal climate of thoughts and feelings. Thoughts and feelings vibrate and attract. In essence, your thoughts and feelings are creating your reality. So notice how you're feeling about the things you are thinking about because this will shed light on the essence you're attracting into your life. And when you know, you then become empowered to make the choices that suit you best.

In all honesty, we have been taking ourselves way too seriously. We have been so focused on manifestation techniques and strategies these days that we've forgotten to just be. But being present and in the flow allows you to do just that. And the cool thing about "being" is that the manifestation of your truest desires becomes a pleasant side-effect of that.

APPLICATION:

In order to joyously fulfill your truest desires you must be in the flow of life, not struggling against it. And being in the flow can be as simple as expressing the essence of who you truly are right now. Understanding your true essence is probably the most important gift you can give yourself, because it is through this understanding that you will naturally feel fulfilled from the inside-out.

Know that your authentic desires are expressions of your truest essence. As such, aligning with the essence of what you desire and who you are at your core, above all else, is what will not only bring you what you love, it will also get you into the flow of who you really are.

Everything comes down to the experience. Anything you desire at its core is really an essence or an experience you want to have. The things, the people, the circumstances are really the vehicles to that experience, but the essence can be expressed in infinitely joyous ways. So to focus only on the means, i.e. on the vehicle, is to ignore the primary factor involved in the manifestation process. It's like ignoring the root of a tree and only focusing on the branches to bear fruit. The essence is what you desire, and this essence is already yours and within you to express right now. It's simply a matter of choice.

So instead of seeking something outside of yourself to bring you joy, be joyful now from within your soul. Stop waiting and start choosing to be happy right now. Then your external manifestations will simply be reflections of your inner truth rather than the sole means of your happiness. Then your happiness will be dependant on you rather than on other people, things, or outside circumstances alone.

So, let's begin. Think of something you dream about doing, having, and/or being. Think about how it would feel to do, have, and/or be it right now. Remember, don't just think about what you want in terms of the things, people, and circumstances in and of themselves. Again, it's the essence of your desires that you are really after, so dwell on the essence of what you love, and if you want, use specific details simply to awaken more of that essence feeling within you. Remember, your aim is to feel this reality right now because you know that you are already one with all you desire. This is not a trick. You are not trying to fool yourself into belief. This is simply an expression of pure truth of which you are reminding yourself.

Next, notice the ways in which the essence you desire is present in your life right now. Focus on it as something you already have within you. This will end up materializing the physical expressions of that essence in the ways that are best for you. Do not get attached to anything specific. Let the essence be your guide and know that there are infinite positive ways this essence can manifest in your life. When you lead with the essence, the details joyously follow; details that are often even better than you ever imagined.

Stay focused on the feeling of the essence you would like to express in your life because feelings help drive your manifestations. They are the energetic fuel that backs your thoughts, words, and actions as they impact the vibration you put out into The Universe. So feel yourself experiencing the essence of wealth, health, love, joy, success, and whatever else you desire. What does that feel like to you? As you continue to feel it, find evidence of this essence in your life right now. Then do what you need to do to stay in this feeling, all the while recognizing the truth of it.

At this point you may be thinking that it's hard to feel the essence of something you don't currently see as present in your life. But know that you can always find a way to feel the essence you wish to express. All you need is some creativity and open-mindedness. So if you don't feel wealthy because you're swimming in debt, think about what wealth really means and find evidence of it all around you. A simple glance at a lawn with its infinite blades of grass, or a lake with its abundance of water, or the wealth of love you feel from a loved-one, will quickly turn you on to the wealth all around you.

It doesn't really matter where you start, just start. Be present and be aware and guaranteed you will find evidence of the essence you seek already within you and all around you. The more you get into the feeling of what you love, and feel proactively grateful for it, the more you will realize that this is who you are and what you have already. So bring yourself into the present and feel the proactive gratitude for what you know is already yours in essence, and soon it will manifest in form and experience as well.

Next, go off and act the part, be the part, act "as if" what you desire is already yours. Express the essence of your desires right now. Be confident in your actions and follow the inspirations you receive. Be as authentic as possible. Be as bold as you feel is necessary, but also know that you don't need to make any rash decisions.

For instance, you don't have to run out right now to buy a new house you don't feel you can afford. You can simply get into the essence feeling of having a home you love. You can go to open houses, drive through neighborhoods, browse through furniture stores, de-clutter your current place to get it move-ready whenever you're ready, and basically do what you would do anyway, i.e. the preparatory steps you would actually take if you were looking for your dream home. Don't worry about the way. By acting the part, by being the part, the way will show up. In the meantime, just enjoy yourself in the moment with joyous abandon. After all, it doesn't cost you anything to dream.

Don't give up on your dreams. Feel them as possibilities and refuse to settle for less than you deserve. With that said, when it comes to big picture goals, stay mindful of the steps along the way and don't be afraid to take steps in the interim that may not yet be exactly what your big picture goal may indicate.

For example, if you have a dream home in mind, that doesn't mean you can't buy another home in the interim. As long as you are not settling out of doubt or lack of faith, you will soon recognize that each step you take is one that's taking you in the direction of where you want to go. So in the meantime, enjoy what you do have and expand from there. Know that your investment now may be the one that leads you to that big picture goal later. Just know the difference between settling for less out of doubt and impatience versus taking steps towards your goals with joy and appreciation for the present moment.

Being in the Flow and Fulfilling Your Desires

Do what feels right to you in the moment. Take inspired action with confidence and faith and remain unattached to the outcome. Take it moment by moment and allow your flow of energy to guide you in the best direction, whatever that may be. Release the pressure and know that step by step you are manifesting your goals in perfect time and order.

Remember that acting "as if" your desires are already a reality in your life can simply be about a change in consciousness too. It's as much about energetic action as it is about physical action. You want to make sure that you are aligned in your thoughts, feelings, beliefs, and subsequent actions so that you are consistent in your point of attraction, and so that you aren't creating resistance to or contradicting what you desire to express. It all starts with your attitude and with your alignment. Your actions will naturally flow from there.

So, for instance, if you want to be in a loving and healthy relationship, feel what that would feel like now and take action from a place of wholeness and trust. Think about how you would behave, what you would do if you were confident in yourself and felt utterly fulfilled. Rather than feeling desperate and discouraged, think about the essence you would be exemplifying, the essence of confidence, security, enjoyment, and the like. Then go out and express those qualities. Be active, do those things you love, feel your inner confidence, and know that this confidence depends on you and no one else. Then you will be a magnet for what you love and desire to express and manifest.

Acting "as if" really refers to being "as if," rather than faking something or pretending. Do not turn what you do into a means to another end (like manifesting something else). Make it about the experience at hand and make that experience your end goal. Then your actions won't be about pretending or faking anything; you will actually be doing what you love in the moment. You will already be feeling and enjoying the essence you desire to manifest without all the pressure to actually manifest it. This is what it means to be in the flow; to be doing what you love while being devoid of worry or stress, to feel like you are already experiencing the joy you seek.

For example, let's say your goal is to feel the essence of wealth. First, realize that you are this essence already. Wealthy is what you are at your core, no matter what your outer appearances may be suggesting. Recognize this and notice this truth as present in your life right now.

Now in order to truly be wealthy you must feel wealthy. So go do something that feels wealthy to you right now, and simply do it for the sake of the experience itself. For example, if you choose to test drive your dream car, do not focus on wanting to manifest your dream car. Rather, test drive it for the sake of the experience of test driving it. That's it. Enjoy the moment you're in and let that be your only goal at that time. Then you will be in the essence and in the flow of what you love and enjoy, without agenda and without attachment.

Now notice and appreciate the wealth that's in your life right now, and then share it. Be happy for the wealth of others too. Also know that wealth moves beyond money, and as such, you are indeed always wealthy in many ways.

Now go out and express your wealth. Give a smile, give a dollar, buy someone a tea, lend a helping hand, take yourself to a nice lunch, browse in your dream store, be in awe of nature, etc. Do all those things that express the wealth that you truly embody right now and always. Remember, wealth is a state of mind. You can be the richest person on earth with all the money you could ever want and still be poor in spirit.

So, acting "as if" is really about embracing who you truly are at your core; the fact that you are already one with everything you could ever desire. It's about taking action on the essence you feel, but taking action that's natural and enjoyable to you. It's about expressing the truth with confidence and not allowing ego-inspired perceptions and appearances to dissuade you. Acting "as if" is simply about feeling authentically good because you know you are already whole right now.

Feeling authentically good means you are in the natural flow of life. To stay there, however, it helps to know the motives behind your desires. As such, whenever you focus on anything, it's important to make sure that you are coming from a place of wholeness rather than lack.

For instance, instead of hoping that something outside of you will make you happy, take action from a perspective of already being happy and complete; from a place where your desire is to express the truth of your abundant nature and the truth of your Infinite Universal Supply. Do it to appreciate creation and to express your truth rather than to artificially fill a perceived void through external means.

Many people seek happiness outside of themselves only to find it still lacking in their lives, even when they seemingly get what they want. To be truly happy and fulfilled you need to start from within, and knowing your motives is a great place to start. So make a list of what you truly want. Then go through that list and ask yourself why you want it. Be honest about this. Doing this exercise will help separate your ego desires from those based in spirit and truth. As you learn about your truest desires, and the motives behind them, you will naturally become more and more aligned with who you truly are. And as you do, you will attract into your life the real fulfillment you seek.

Understand that if we don't question our motives at the forefront, sometimes we won't know how we truly feel about a desire until after it has manifested. The reason for this is because we often get so caught up in the wanting of it that we forget why, or even if, we wanted it in the first place.

For example, sometimes when a relationship ends we find ourselves wanting to get back together. But if we do not assess our motives before hand we may end up wasting a lot of time and energy over something we don't really even want. For instance, perhaps in your desire to rekindle the relationship all you really want is closure, validation, ego gratification, respect, or simply to be heard. Maybe you're feeling lonely in the moment and you think this relationship will solve that problem.

So if you assess why you actually want to reconnect you may realize that what you really want is not the relationship itself, but rather, another outcome altogether. Subsequently, by being present and aware you'll become conscious of your actual desire, and in the process, you'll save yourself a lot of heartache and struggle that would have likely resulted from chasing after something you didn't even want. You'll finally know what you actually desire, which will help you ask for what you really want and need, without causing confusion to you or to others.

So think about why you want what you want before you spend your time focusing on it and even pursuing it. Imagine yourself getting it. What would that feel like? Can you feel what you really want out of the situation, i.e. the essence of it? Does it also correspond to the thing, person, or circumstance you thought you wanted, or are you desiring another effect or experience altogether?

Going through this process will help you focus accurately on what you authentically desire in the moment, which will prevent you from wasting time chasing after something false. And know that even if it is the thing, person, or circumstance that you want, if it doesn't want you, then it's simply not for you at this time. Knowing this will again help you reassess your desires, let go of what no longer serves you, and then focus on what's best for you instead.

Now, once you are familiar with what you truly desire in life and why, take a few moments to feel what it would feel like to totally let go, to totally surrender your desires to Divine Order. What does that feel like to you? How does your body respond to this notion? Notice if you feel more relaxed, at peace, and less pressured to perform. If you take a few moments each day to meditate on this concept of surrender you will naturally find yourself becoming more and more aligned with your truth and with the guidance that is available to you in each moment. Naturally you will release the struggle and embrace ease, joy, and flow into your life instead.

Also, learn to be patient. We all have our own timelines in which we would like things to happen, and usually it's sooner rather than later. But staying patient and knowing that there is a Divine Order to everything will help you release any attachments and desperation you might have, and help prevent the unnecessary slow down of your manifestation process. Know that if your desires are not manifesting, you're either not aligned with them or the timing just isn't right yet. And you'll know which it is by noticing your level of resistance to what you want.

When you think about what you authentically desire, what feelings come up? Are you feeling excited and faithful, or are you feeling hopeless and doubtful? If you are doubtful and you feel resistance whenever you think about what you truly want, then you know you are delaying the manifestation of it needlessly through your own blocking of it. But, if you are feeling patient and enthused and you are aligned with it in thought, feeling, belief, and action, then just be patient and trust that all is manifesting in perfect time and order for you.

If at any time you are feeling desperate or impatient just remember to trust in Divine Order. Stop yourself from interfering with the process by choosing to let go of your own timelines, doubts, and agendas and by choosing to trust in the guidance you receive. Believing that everything has its reason and that all is for the best will help you let go of your attachments to the way you think things "should be," and embrace infinite trust and patience instead. So if you're ever feeling any resistance towards your desires, simply work on changing your beliefs and the resistance will disappear.

Know that in order to receive what you've been "asking for" you need to be aligned with it energetically. But on a deeper level, knowing your motives for your desires will help you align with those that are most authentic to you. So next time you're wondering what's the hold up, first ask yourself why you want what you want, and then follow it up with how you really feel about having it.

Finally, know that one of the quickest ways to get what you desire is to give it, because doing this puts you in alignment with Infinite Abundance and Flow. When you give what you want to receive you indicate a sense of trust and faith and generosity that ultimately leads you to your own fulfillment, naturally and joyously. By giving what you love the most, by sharing the essence of what you want to receive, you invoke the law of attraction to work in your favor. By focusing on someone else's needs for just a moment, you end up displaying a sense of trust and faith and confidence in The Universe to take care of your needs. By helping someone else achieve their dreams you end up transforming your own desperation into something proactive and useful instead. In truth, it is through sharing that you ultimately end up in the flow of life and truly fulfilled.

Chapter 23:
Being in the Flow and Creating Alignment

The Universe's precise alignment enables all of life to flourish in perfect order.

Being in the flow is really about being aligned with your core. At your core you are not lacking anything. On the surface of your awareness your ego might beg to differ, but in truth, the only reason you ever feel lack in your life is because you are not aligned with the truth. Understand that your awareness and alignment are what matter most to your success, more so than any exertion of effort you could ever offer on your part. Yes, action of some sort is often required, but it is the action that comes of aligned thinking and aligned feeling that really puts you into the flow of things.

When you are aware of and fully engaged in the present moment this is when you are truly in the flow of life and aligned with your true nature of total well-being. It is in this state that you are open and aware, and as such, your core desires are free to materialize in the best ways simply because you are no longer blocking them through your resistance. When you are concentrated on the moment at hand, and you are positive about it, any resistance in your life just dissolves away, leaving you open to the flow of good that is yours to receive.

When you are aligned with authentic happiness, and the truth of your infinite joy and abundance, you can trust that The Universe is always delivering the best for you. The Universe simply reflects your own core desires, values, and overall consciousness. It inspires you and it guides you based on your purpose. So when you are aligned with your truth, everything you desire is aligned with your truth too. If you just learn to let go of your ego, trust your true instincts, and take inspired action in each moment with your purpose and passion in mind, everything else will become clear to you. You will know what to do, when to do it, and how to do it, when the time is right.

Being in the flow is about aligning with the Energy Source from which all emanates. In every moment you have a choice, you can either align with the truth, or you can choose to fall into negative beliefs. But if you choose alignment, you will then be able to easily release the struggle and embrace joy in your life instead. You will be able to let go and allow yourself to be guided to inspired action. You will be able to enjoy your life, be authentically happy, and allow your fulfillment to manifest from the inside-out.

At the end of the day, it's all about being authentic and making choices from a place of authentic happiness and truth. Focusing on alignment, then, simply means feeling and embracing the essence of who you truly are, now and always. You are joy, you are well-being, you are wealth, you are love, you are peace of mind, and you are all things that you consider to be good. All you need to do for this to manifest in your life is to acknowledge that this is already who you are right now. It's simply a matter of embracing your true identity and then choosing to express that truth in your most authentic ways. Then as you focus your attention on these truths, they will naturally flow to you as joyous manifestations.

Declare your true and natural state and notice how everything else effortlessly falls into place. Notice how your external world starts to mirror your new awareness as you get deeper and deeper into the truth of who you really are. Notice how your thoughts, feelings, beliefs, and actions all align to match your new found consciousness.

Focus on your alignment first and foremost, then let go and enjoy each moment, one after another. Trust that what you authentically want, and what's right for you, also wants you, and that's why you want it in the first place. Know that struggle is not required to fulfill your purpose and total joy. All you need is to find your flow and let it carry you. This is not a passive approach by any means. Rather, it's an awareness that in each moment your choices are determining your level of alignment, and subsequently, what manifests into your life. It's simply a matter of allowing yourself to be led by your soul versus your ego, and then taking action that is most aligned with your truth.

The more aligned you are with your true and natural state, the more aligned you will be with the joyous flow of life. But the degree of your alignment centers on your level of awareness. So the more aware you are of the truth, the more aligned you will be with it, and the more easily you will enjoy flow in your life. To illustrate further, here are some levels of awareness briefly laid out:

1. At the first level of awareness you go through life as a victim of circumstance, feeling like you have no control and believing in randomness. Here you feel helpless. You blame others for your lack of success in life. You feel resentful and jealous. Your happiness is constantly dependant on what's going on in your external world. You are constantly reacting to what's happening to you, and never aware of your role in creating it. You are manifesting based on an auto-pilot program by which your subconscious mind is being led by your fears, your insecurities, your negative beliefs, and the like.

    Here you are not aware of or do not believe in Universal Laws, so you go about your life in a reactive state of mind that's driven solely or mostly by your ego. You live in a victim mentality, rarely or never achieving what you truly desire in life. You also never have a shortage of complaints or scapegoats. And even if you do achieve what you think you want (or likely what your ego wants), you still feel empty inside but don't know why.

2. At the next level of awareness you understand the nature of The Universe and Universal Laws and use them consciously to get what you want. Here you understand how empowered you really are to

manifest the reality of your choosing. Here you know you can pretty much be, do, and have in essence anything you desire. Here you use deliberate focus as a means of assisting you in manifesting your desires. But here you may or may not be aware of the distinction between your true desires and those of your ego.

3. At the next level of awareness you are in a more advanced state of consciousness where you know the difference between your authentic desires and your ego's desires, and you choose only to pursue those that are authentic to you. Here you use the power of deliberate focus mostly to align with the truth of your infinite nature and to release all your doubts and resistance. While you may use deliberate focus to manifest specific desires, here you understand the importance of consciousness and so you do your best to firstly work through your subconscious beliefs to ensure that they are aligned with your true self and what your true self really wants.

    At this level you understand the importance of knowing your motives because you know that motive is what ultimately affects the quality of what you receive. You know that as long as your desires are based in purpose, love, and truth, rather than ego, you will attract not only what you love, but also what is right for you.

4. At the next level of awareness you have a feeling of total trust and connection to a higher purpose and you allow yourself to surrender to this purpose, which you know will always bring you total fulfillment. Here you know you can be, do, and have essentially anything you desire, but you choose to follow the guidance you receive to what your soul really wants to express, and you trust that whatever that is, it's something you will always find ultimately fulfilling and enjoyable.

    At this level you don't feel the need to be so intentional or deliberate with your focus because you are already aligned with the truth of your being and your purpose. You know that manifesting your fulfillment will ultimately come from your alignment anyway so while you can focus on specifics, you don't feel the need to. Here your goal is simply to be a successful channel through which The Universe does its work, and as such, whatever manifests and whatever you are inspired to do you trust will always be for the best.

Now, this doesn't mean that at this level you never set intentions or have specific focus or goals. It simply means that your intentions, focus, and desires come to you naturally via your alignment with your true self. It means you don't feel the need to force, push, or manipulate your focus because it already comes to you as something organic and authentic to you. It means that you are easily able to detach from the specifics and outcome of things because you totally trust in Divine Order.

At this level of awareness your purpose drives you and you allow yourself to be guided from moment to moment to what is best for you rather than trying to control every detail. You never worry about what's next or whether or not you'll like it. You never doubt your inspirations, and as such, you take inspired action with confidence and joy. At this level you are able to be still enough to hear the whispers of your soul, and then take action on what you're guided to do. You are aware that you are one with creation and that you have everything within you to manifest naturally what's best and most fulfilling for you. You are able to trust in your purpose and follow it with faith and joy. As such, you are purpose-driven and peaceful in your actions, feeling relaxed, certain, and happy at all times. Consequently, everything just flows to you effortlessly and joyously. You can simply live in the moment and enjoy the present as the gift that it is.

Understand that being in the flow is ultimately about reaching and staying in the highest level of consciousness where you are totally aligned with the truth behind All There Is. However, it is not uncommon for most of us to jump between these levels of awareness from time to time. But the more we focus on alignment, rather than manifestation alone, the more we will be in the higher state of consciousness where everything we love just flows effortlessly and joyously to us. This is where your higher-self resides. This is where your truth lives. This is who you really are at your core. The more you stay in this awareness, the smoother and more enjoyable your life will be.

Deliberate focus at any stage is not a bad idea. Even in the latter stage of higher consciousness there's nothing wrong with visualizing outcomes that feel authentically good to you. It's simply a matter of staying detached from desperation and then surrendering to a Divine Order. It's a matter of affirming your truths and your intentions, feeling their essence in the moment, and then letting go and allowing your purpose to lead the way. The key is to use your present moments to ensure that while you may have your ideas as to what you want, you are also able to surrender those ideas to Source to deliver what's ultimately in your best interest.

Many people have it backwards. They have a desire, whether authentic or not, and they actively pursue it through intense action. They set goals and timelines and act upon them at all costs. They push, struggle, chase, and worry, which all cause stress and struggle. They get so attached to one outcome that they either pressure their goals into manifesting (but end up feeling empty anyway), or they get so tired and discouraged that they end up giving up altogether.

But there's a better process. This process is not about being passive or apathetic. This process is about being truly inspired and fulfilled. This process is about being in the flow. It's where you allow yourself to be still enough to hear your true calling. It's where you follow your intuition and internal guidance system. It's where your main focus is on aligning with Source Energy through authentic joy, and then allowing your thoughts, feelings, desires, focus, and actions to sprout naturally from that alignment. It's where you have total trust and faith in the process of life and you allow it to carry you effortlessly and joyously in every moment to where you need to be and to what you need to do.

Know that by staying aligned with the core of who you are you open yourself up to opportunities and revelations in all areas of your life. You start to understand where you may be blocking yourself and how you can fix it. Simply stated, when you are aligned from within you empower yourself to live the life you love by creating a positive momentum that inevitably runs through every area of your life.

So pay attention to the overall essence of your focus, as well as your overall feelings, attitudes, and beliefs to see how authentically aligned you really are with your truth, your joy, and your intentions. Check in with yourself from time to time on a daily basis to make sure you are drawing to yourself what you truly love and enjoy rather than what is inauthentic to you and ultimately unfulfilling. Notice the beliefs you hold about what you think you can and cannot be, do, and have, and then positively transform those beliefs that contradict your intentions. And if you feel out of alignment, do your best to focus on anything positive to help bring you back into it. That way you will be continuing the positive momentum that's actively creating overall harmony in your life right now.

Keep in mind as well that while alignment can come from the enjoyment and appreciation of external circumstances, like for instance receiving love from someone or getting a raise, alignment needs to also be something you can cultivate in the moment without any external reason. We can certainly find many external reasons to be happy, and therefore aligned, but it's important that we are also able to tap into our alignment at any time, including and especially when we've lost our way.

It's important that you feel happy from within and that you don't completely rely on external factors to provide you with your happiness. Instead, be happy for no particular reason. Meaning, be happy as your way of being. Be happy because you know that you are one with Infinite Love, Infinite Joy, and Infinite Abundance. Let your overall attitude be of proactive appreciation, not just for the physical things and experiences in your life that are favorable to you, but also for the simple sake of being who you are and knowing where you come from; from knowing you are full of joyous possibilities. Then what will happen is that your external circumstances will become a reflection of your internal state of happiness, alignment, and appreciation rather than the sole cause of your joy.

Finally, know that if you want something it has to want you back. This is what alignment is all about. You cannot attract something with which you are not aligned. So focus on your authentic alignment first and foremost and you will be assured of total fulfillment from the inside-out.

APPLICATION:

Being in the flow is about staying in alignment so that you allow your good to unfold. It's about recognizing your inherent nature and your oneness with All There Is. It's about being aware of the guidance you are receiving, and using that inspiration to make proactive and aligned choices in how you choose to think, feel, believe, and act now, and in each moment.

Being in the flow leads you to the manifestation of your true and total fulfillment, naturally and without struggle. As such, it's best to direct your focus on aligning yourself with this flow rather than just trying to manifest anything specific.

Start by assessing your level of awareness. Be honest about what you truly believe, and where it has gotten you thus far. Go through the levels of awareness previously outlined and figure out where you stand. Then, every day, work on getting yourself into a higher and higher state of consciousness. But don't be too hard on yourself either. Move at your own pace and be compassionate with yourself along the way.

Then focus on being appreciative. In fact, appreciation is one of the fastest ways to align yourself with Universal Energy, and subsequently, with joy and fulfillment. Acknowledge what you have to be grateful for right now. You can start with anything. Every moment gives you a chance to enjoy and appreciate something about your life. And as you do, you will naturally fall more and more into alignment with the fulfillment you've always wanted to experience.

When you are appreciative by nature you step onto an energetic wave that holds all the fulfillment you could ever want in life. So stay in the zone of proactive appreciation and your soul's desires will materialize in the most joyous and peaceful ways. But remember to always be genuine.

Every day think of what you appreciate about your life. You can start by listing things from your external world. For example, you could say that you are grateful for your home, your job, your vacation, your family, your health, etc. But then go deeper. Recognize the gratitude you have for your sense of comfort, stability, joy, security, love, prosperity, and so on. This is about getting to the essence, to the core. By doing so you will be well on your way to aligning with the essence of who you truly are. Also, be grateful for what you want in advance. Know it's a possibility for you to be more successful, healthier, stronger, more joyous, or whatever the case may be, and then feel that gratitude now.

Know that what you see on the outside is a direct reflection of what's happening on the inside. Know that you are always abundant in essence, and the way to see that materialize in your life is to simply acknowledge it as being true. Then take inspired action that's aligned with that awareness and watch as everything naturally and joyously unfolds.

Appreciate each moment and each step along your path because each one has its own merit and message. Trust that everything is manifesting in the perfect time and in the perfect way and then simply go on and enjoy your life. Be open to the synchronicities and opportunities that are being provided for you, even if they seem different from what you had imagined or expected. Trust that each step and each moment is taking you to where you need to be.

Alignment is about feeling infinitely connected to All There Is. It's about knowing that you can be, do, and have in essence anything you desire. It's about trusting in your authentic desires and allowing yourself to dream big without letting fear, doubt, or attachment get in your way. So when you get a positive idea about something you want to be, do, and/or have, do not dismiss it, do not reject it. Trust that it is there for a reason. Feel it as your truth right now. Feel it as your reality right now. Find the essence behind it, feel that essence, and notice this essence in your life right now.

If at any time you feel out of alignment, consciously choose thoughts and feelings and actions that bring you back into it. Rather than trying to manifest something specific, simply choose these thoughts, feelings, and actions because they are aligned with who you really are, and because they just feel so authentically good.

At any point if you feel that you're pushing, stop. Stop swimming against the current. Trust that what's best for you will flow with ease as long as you align with your core and your truth. If you feel yourself struggling at any point, just surrender, let go, and move on. Trust that what is best is manifesting for you right now. Understand that the longer you stay stuck in the pushing and forcing and desperate wanting of things, the more you will prevent what's really good for you from showing up.

Alignment is about understanding that you attract that which matches your vibrational offering (your energy). You cannot receive something with which you are not a match. So don't struggle, don't push, and don't try to force something to be. Just focus on being aligned with your truth and trust that whatever manifests (or doesn't) out of that truth is all for the best.

So how can you tell if you're aligned with your truth or not? Well, one great way of realizing how aligned you really are in every area of your life is to assess how you feel about each area, and then to notice the level of success you've experienced respectfully. That is, notice if your truest desires have been manifesting with ease, or if you've been finding it hard to manifest what you truly love. As it stands, what are your present circumstances telling you about your frame of mind?

For example, think about what you've been thinking, feeling, and doing with respect to those areas in your life that have been working for you, i.e. those things that just seem to flow with ease and joy and in a totally synchronized way. Where has your consciousness been with respect to these things? What actions have you been taking?

Now think the same about the areas where you are still waiting on your manifestations. What patterns are you repeating that keep bringing you to the same unfulfilling place over and over again?

Notice the habits you've established with both your successes and your "failures." Then by understanding what methods have worked and what haven't you can adjust your alignment accordingly in the present to create the best results for your present and for your future alike.

Chapter 24:
Being in the Flow and Fulfilling Your Purpose

Look closely and you will see that everything in one way or another is meant to be.

Being in the flow, being aligned, and fulfilling your desires is simply about living your life with purpose. In fact, purpose is what ultimately drives your truest desires in the first place, so what you love is really no coincidence at all. As you focus your attention on truth, love, and infinite abundance in the moment, all the details of your purpose will come to you naturally and without you having to dictate them to The Universe. You can simply do what you love and love what you do and the rest will take care of itself.

You must trust in your core desires and in the essence you wish to express because your purpose often speaks to you through these desires. It tells you who you really are and what you already have within you to manifest. There truly is a reason for why you want what you want in life. Do not reject your passions in favor of "common sense," because to reject passion is to reject your own destiny of total fulfillment, and the potential benefit you can provide to the world.

You have the free will to choose whether you're in the flow or not. You have the free will to choose whether you follow your purposeful path or you follow the one of your ego. But if you want to be ultimately fulfilled, your best bet is to honor your soul's desires by questioning those of your ego. Your best bet is to believe in your ability to manifest the essence of what you truly desire with ease and joy because you know it's yours already.

You Are Here

To ensure you always manifest what is most authentic to your soul, instead of strictly focusing on what you want and then attempting to manifest it from there, focus on who you are at your core. Start with your alignment with your true self and with the essence you want to express rather than attaching yourself to specifics. Start with focusing on your true identity, your purpose, your oneness with Source, and your true nature that is all-loving, trusting, and infinitely abundant. Trust that as you align with this truth, the rest of the details will effortlessly show up.

Understand that manifesting true fulfillment is less about getting clear about what you want, and more about getting clear about who you are. You attract based on who you are so it would make sense to focus on aligning with your true self before you think about manifesting anything specific. Otherwise you will be attracting things inauthentic to you, which will only perpetuate any dissatisfaction you may be experiencing. So focus on being your best self and on aligning yourself with your core, your purpose, and your truth. And then release any false expectations you've placed on yourself based on external pressures and the opinions of others.

There is definitely something happening beneath the surface driving us to what we love and want, but often we aren't present enough in the moment to hear that guidance. So instead we listen to common opinion and our egos telling us what we "should" want. We compete with others not realizing that what they want may not even be what we really want for ourselves.

But if we let go of all of that, if we let go of the deliberation and intentionality for just a moment, we will be able to hear our guidance to what is real and true. If you take your focus off of the rat race for just one moment, you may actually become clear as to what you really want and who you really are. Then you will be able to set and let go of your intentions with confidence, knowing they are for you to manifest.

If you let it, your purpose will guide you to what you truly love and enjoy. Your ego may try to distract you from this purpose, but you needn't listen. It's important that you do what you authentically love, not just something you think is desirable because you've seen the success and fame it has brought others. You are here to fully express your own truth, not imitate someone else's. It's fine to be inspired by others' successes, but let your own path reveal to you your personal success, instead of chasing after something that just isn't right for you.

Your destiny is to share your unique perspective of life with the world. Everyone adds value, and you are no different. You are important and you are here for a reason. You are no bigger and no smaller than anyone else. While what you do may or may not appear glamorous or important in the eyes of others, know that it too is important to the collective goal. Just be true to yourself and you will find true fulfillment in every moment of your life.

Trust that there is no one out there exactly like you. While some of us may have similar ambitions, in reality we are all truly unique in that each of us has our own purpose to fulfill in our own special way. Each of us represents a specific piece of the overall puzzle and so our importance must not be underestimated. Some may have bigger fish to fry, but that doesn't make anyone else any less important or valuable. We all have our unique purpose in life. Focus on yours.

Don't let your self-esteem and identity depend on whether or not you feel better or worse off than others because that sort of comparison will only take you farther away from your own purpose in life. So just be. Be your best and do your best and know that it's more than good enough. If you're going to compete with anyone, compete with yourself to surpass your own perceived limitations rather than wasting your time comparing yourself to others and feeling inadequate. Use the successes of others to inspire you but then go out and do your own thing.

You are gifted with your own talents and core desires for a reason. Following through on them will not only benefit you, it will also benefit all those who will be touched by your gifts and inspired by your actions. The Universe always functions on a win-win basis. Know this as you proceed through life, and know that while there is an infinite pool of possibilities out there, there are possibilities that simply fit you best.

You can be, do, and have in essence anything you desire in this world, and you can express it all in your own unique way, but you needn't compare yourself to others. Let others do what they came here to do, and let yourself do what you came here to do. Don't get lost in the chase for something your ego thinks is better. Trust in your own path, in your own inspirations, and in your own purpose. Let your purpose be the star of your movie, guiding you to your best fulfillment, which will subsequently be what's best for all.

Allow your focus to come naturally from guidance and then take inspired action accordingly with trust and faith. Then your intentions will be filled with purpose and surrender, which is the perfect formula for the manifestation of true fulfillment. You must trust that as you align with your authentic nature your purpose will do the rest, inspiring you to do what you love most. Then Divine Guidance will send you the right people and opportunities that will fit in perfectly with your personal bliss.

Let your passions be your guide, and the rest will flow with joy and ease. Let your focus be on providing value, and your success will come naturally and in ways that are most fulfilling for you. Your ego wants you to believe that there's only one path to success, and that you must chase after it at all costs. But this is not the case. In fact, the more you chase after something inauthentic to you, the unhappier you will become, and the more struggle and dissatisfaction you will likely endure no matter how much you accumulate or achieve.

Let yourself be inspired by Divine Intelligence and by your higher-self as to what you truly desire at your core and what's truly aligned with your purpose and total joy. Get present and still and listen to the voice of your inner calling, to the inspiration of Divine Guidance, and to the wisdom of The Universe speaking to you and through you. Your ego has its own concept of what it thinks will "make you happy," and it's always wrong in the end. Follow your soul's calling and you will know what true happiness means. Know that the more you chase after an illusion, the less aligned you will be with what you are really meant to do, be, and have.

Being in the Flow and Fulfilling Your Purpose

Your purpose is not something you need to chase after or struggle to find. All you need to do is align with the truth of Infinite Love, Infinite Joy, Infinite Abundance, and all good, and then your purpose will naturally come to the surface of your awareness. As soon as you can control your ego and stop resisting your true self your purpose will find you, or rather, it will reveal itself to you. Your purpose is something that is always with you. All you need is to open yourself up to realizing that.

You are gifted with free will and because of that you get to choose your path in life. But know that no matter what you choose, there is always a purpose behind it. Even choices made from your ego have lessons to be learned. So simply be aware of your choices and find meaning in their consequences and you will be empowered to manifest the purposeful life you love.

It's not about chasing after your purpose, forcing your purpose to be something that it's not, or trying to copy someone else because you feel what they're doing is more important or more glamorous. It's about being true to yourself and knowing that what you have to offer is of great value too. It's about being present and aware of the choices you're making in life and adding consciousness to each one.

Being in the flow is about being aligned with your purpose and surrendering your desires to flow naturally. If you let it, your heart will speak to you and tell you what you truly want to know. Focus on being a successful vehicle through which Source Energy works. Know that The Universe will respond to your heart's desires if you simply stop resisting them. Align yourself with the truth right now and you will know what it means to live a life of purpose, joy, and total flow.

APPLICATION:

You are here to fulfill your purpose, to be fulfilled, to manifest the essence of anything you desire (preferably purposeful), and subsequently to share your joy with the world. At your core you know this, along with how to get it done. But it's up to you to align with this intention through recognizing the truth of who you really are and why you're really here.

But purpose tends to hide from those who are pre-occupied with life and blocking themselves through false desires, impressions, and identities. This is not to say that what you're currently doing is not important. You still need to pay your bills and take care of your home and finish projects and work, and so on. It's just that we often get so caught up in our everyday routines and in unnecessary distractions that we forget to look inside ourselves for answers.

Do not put your passions on the backburner. Trust that they are trying to tell you something. Rather than ignoring them, seize the moment and do something with them instead. Take time to appreciate what you love and to put passion into all that you do. Then you will be infusing all that you do with your purpose too.

Don't think you have time? That's nonsense because you can find purpose everywhere; in the mundane and in the extraordinary. It's all a matter of perception. It's only when you get lost in the images of what others are doing or what you think you "should be" doing, that you end up devaluing what you're actually doing.

Your purpose is with you and within you at all times. You do not need to chase it. All you need to do is get present enough with yourself to notice it. It's been peaking out from time to time, sending you messages and giving you direction. Have you been listening?

Purpose is multi-dimensional and inter-connected. It's about who you are, what you do, who you meet, what you learn, what you teach, and so on. That's why to align with it is to align with your total fulfillment, because as you express the truth of who you are and where you come from, you will be naturally fulfilling your joyous destiny too.

Being in the Flow and Fulfilling Your Purpose

Now, if you already feel purpose in your life, at least to some degree, that's great. But know that it may be more dynamic than you yet know. Understand that purpose is not just about your job. Purpose is something that permeates every aspect of your life. It's who you are in every moment. But whether you think you know or you don't, here are some steps you can take to help you figure out your purpose:

1. Take time each day to get quiet and think about absolutely nothing. This may be challenging at first but with practice it will get easier. Visualize a white screen, like the one at the movie theatre, and just stare at it in your mind's eye. As images or thoughts come creeping in, brush them off the screen. Do this for a few minutes and notice how much calmer and relaxed you feel.

2. After you've practiced thinking about nothing for a few minutes, next, take notice of any inspirations that come to you. Do you have any strong feelings or visions about what you would enjoy doing the most? If so, don't question them or deny them. Just let them be and see what comes of it. If nothing comes to you at first, do not get discouraged. Instead, think of your hobbies, your passions, things you are exceptionally good at, and things you've always dreamed of doing. Think of the topics that interest you most. By taking note of what you love and allowing yourself to think about it without interference, you then open yourself up to experiencing more passion and more guidance in your life.

3. Now think of all the ways you can share what you love. How can doing what you love not only bring value and fulfillment into your own life, but also into the lives of others? Once again, know that expressing your purpose isn't only about what you do; it's about expressing who you are. Every moment is a chance to be authentic. Every moment gives you an opportunity to share your energy with the world. So think of the values you respect the most, and then live them in your everyday life with everything you do and everyone you meet. So if you value friendship, be a good friend. If you value

honesty and integrity, be that way towards others. Give what you want to receive and you will be infusing purpose into all of your activities; you will be living a purposeful and authentic life.

4. Next, release your doubts and fears. Yes, you can have it all. You can be wealthy and healthy and loved and successful and inspired and relaxed and happy. You can have all of that. And the best part is that everybody benefits. Don't settle for less than you deserve by doubting this. Don't allow your fears to dissuade you from living your purpose, and subsequently, from living your greatest life. Know that you can have it all. You can be your best self and have that reflect in your work, in your home life, in your relationships, in your health, in your wealth, and in all areas of your life. Simply make the conscious choice not to settle for less than you know is possible. Start by doing something you love every day, and then make every moment into one of love, joy, and purpose. Then you will be aligned, in the flow, and totally fulfilled, living a purposeful and joyous life in the most authentic of ways.

Chapter 25:

No Limits

If you don't want to be limited, stop setting limits.

Once upon a time it was commonly believed that the earth was flat, and anyone who disagreed with that "fact" was considered a lunatic. But we all found out how that turned out. Think about it, what are you denouncing or deeming impossible today that will become the common knowledge of tomorrow? What truth and subsequent benefit are you closing yourself off from now because of your reluctance to listen and learn?

When you open up your mind and heart you can't help but realize that there are no limits to the essence of what you can be, do, and have. Your point of power is always in the present moment, and your awareness of that is what will propel you to succeed at anything you authentically desire in life.

Understand that your supply of joy and fulfillment is infinite and it can express itself in an infinite amount of blissful ways. Know that there are endless opportunities awaiting you right now; opportunities for understanding, for learning, for sharing, for enjoying, for appreciating, for transforming, and simply for being happy.

Do not get stuck in insecurities, fears, or worries, and don't let the past dictate your future either. Every moment is a clean slate, ready and awaiting your creative input. The future to you is endless in possibilities, so dream big right now knowing that anything you purely desire is within your reach. Stay certain, stay faithful, and stay optimistic.

Understand that everything you could ever desire already exists now as energy, as potential, and even as physical expressions. All you need to do is recognize this energetic presence within you and trust that the essence of what you love will naturally manifest for you in the best ways. So connect with your infinite nature right now. Trust that your purpose and ultimate fulfillment are your birthright. And know that the only one who can stop you from living the life you desire and love is you.

Realizing your infinite nature gives you the freedom to dream big and to fulfill your deepest desires without reservations. It frees you of fear and doubt and allows you to feel happy, whole, and complete because you know that there's truly nothing that you lack. As a result, you can feel confident, capable of anything, and appreciative for who you are and what you have right now, while also feeling free to manifest your full potential in each moment.

Knowing that your point of power is always in the now, you can freely explore your desires and ambitions without setting limits on what you can accomplish. Because you are not using past experiences to dictate what you can and cannot do, and because you are not dwelling on fear, you are then free to simply be your best self, and be, do, and have in essence anything you desire.

But can you really be, do, and have anything you want? Is this "realistic"? Well, in truth, at the core of anything you desire lies an essence, and it's really the essence you are after more than anything else. Think about it, do you want money, or do you want financial freedom and security? Do you want a fit body, or do you want health and self-esteem? So ask yourself, "What is the essence behind what I want?" "What feeling and experience am I looking to receive?"

You can be, do, and have the essence of anything you desire because you already have it within you. So break your desire down to its essence, and then choose to experience that essence right now. Know that you can experience the essence of anything you want whenever you want simply by placing your attention on it and feeling it in the moment. And know that by doing so you will ultimately bring the best manifestation of it to you naturally.

Anyway, the real question needs to be less about whether or not you can manifest what you desire, and more about why you want to. Knowing your motives and ensuring that they are authentic will actually help you positively affect the outcome of whatever it is that you do. It will determine the types of experiences you will end up manifesting, and it will determine your level of true happiness too. So be mindful of why you want what you want, and why you do what you do, for it's in this knowledge that you will find the key to your true fulfillment.

In truth, when you are aligned with your authenticity you are never really inspired to do something, be something, or have something you cannot do, be, or have. Sure there are endless possibilities to tap into, but there are also specific ones that are most fitted to you. As such, your authentic desires are inspiring you to follow your own purpose. So seek to align with your purpose and you will be able to be, do, and have in essence anything you desire because it is already yours. And know that when you are aligned with your purpose you are truly infinite and unlimited in what you can accomplish because you have The Infinite Universe at your back, moving you forward in the most loving of ways. So believe in yourself and act accordingly with purpose and joy in all areas of your life.

Understand, however, that you cannot be limitless if you are setting limits and blocking your own success. If you are insecure and doubtful, if you feel you are undeserving, if you hide behind walls and masks, that's exactly what will be reflected back to you in your life. You need to release your blockages and realize that every moment is a new opportunity for you to do and be something great. Each moment gives you a chance to express your true self. You are truly renewed and full of potential in every moment. If you allow your fears, your doubts, or your past to dictate your future you will be wasting your present moments by filling them up with something that no longer serves you.

When you realize that each moment is unlimited in its possibilities and bound by nothing you will start believing in yourself and what you can be, do, and have. You are unlimited and dynamic; all you need to do is to accept that as fact. No one is standing in the way of you and your greatest life. Only you can stand in your own way, so stop creating self-imposed limitations that aren't based in any truth at all, and start living the life you love and deserve.

Know that your circumstances right now do not define or limit you. They are simply expressions of your past consciousness. So change your consciousness now and eventually you will also change your circumstances. You are only limited by your own belief in limitation. But if you trust that your true nature is infinite and whole, you will act accordingly as a limitless being, and you will manifest the results to match.

Beliefs of limited supply, incompleteness, and lack are all born of the ego; they are not real. So in order to manifest your full potential you need to keep your beliefs aligned with truth, and then take action accordingly. Take action as if it were impossible for you to fail. In spite of your doubts, go for your dreams and see what happens. Even if you fear failure, go for it anyway, you might just surprise yourself and you might just learn something. Remember, your life is about your journey and your experiences, not just the end result.

Understand that The Universe never says no. It is an all-giving Source that will deliver to you what you ask. It simply responds to your energetic output (your thoughts, feelings, beliefs, and actions), so it is up to you to make sure that your energy is traveling in the right direction. What you offer energetically is what you will get back, plain and simple.

Nothing interferes with your free will. This is your gift and it helps you learn and grow. So it is up to you to align with the essence of what you truly love, and subsequently, what you know is yours already. There is an Ultimate and Infinite Power that's available to you right now; it's within you and all around you in every moment. It's always helping you in all that you do, but in order for it to do so you must accept it and allow it into your life. Then you too will come into your limitless self and be able to express that in every moment of your life.

APPLICATION:

Ask yourself, "If there were no limits to what I could do, be, and have, what would I choose to do right now?" "If I had all the money, time, resources, confidence I could ever want and need, a limitless supply, what would I do with it?" Then, think about why you want what you want. Are you inspired by purpose or solely by ego?

Next, notice the beliefs you are holding with respect to your deservingness and your ability to actually have what you want, because this will uncover any subconscious chatter that may be blocking you from fulfilling your dreams. If you don't feel that you deserve it, and if you are chronically pessimistic about the possibility of having it, you may end up preventing it from showing up, or getting some version of it that still doesn't feel right or bring you the ultimate happiness you seek.

So, once you've determined your truest soul-inspired desires, and once you've realized how vast your potential truly is, fully feel your desires as you experience their manifestation in your mind, heart, and soul. Visualize yourself doing, being, and/or having that which you desire, but let it flow naturally and without force. Feel the essence right now. Let the feeling be the goal and fully engage in it as you experience it in the present moment. Have fun with it.

As you get deeper and deeper into the feeling of infinite possibilities, feel the Life Force Energy moving through you. Feel your connection to Divine Order and your oneness with The Universe. Recognize how you are made of the same raw material as everything else. That is, know that you are made of energy and notice how everything and everyone else you see around you is also made of the same energy. Feel your oneness with it all. Know that it's all and we're all interconnected.

Now take this perspective, knowledge, and feeling with you into the world and freely express your passions without worrying about how everything will turn out. Know that you are one with Divine Love/Divine Abundance/Divine Intelligence, and as such, you have it in you to reach and even surpass your greatest potential.

You Are Here

When in doubt, look around you and realize that everything you see started as a point in consciousness, as energy. Everything is of energy, and energy is infinite in supply. Energy can never run out; it simply transmutes itself. Use that awareness to connect with your Infinite Supply, and as such, to take action knowing that the truth of your being is always abundant, free, and truly limitless. Take a leap of faith and see the delight that ensues. Be present in each moment with the truth in mind and watch as your truest desires become your reality in the most joyous of ways.

Epilogue

The power of presence is not to be underestimated. It is something we all need to recognize and implement into our lives. As we do, we will increasingly become more patient, more loving, more successful, and overall happier than we could have ever imagined.

We needn't get lost in the pressures that are imposed upon us or those we impose upon ourselves, i.e. the pressures that tell us to be more, do more, and have more. We need not worry about the future. We need not obsess about the past. All we need to do to get our power back is to get grounded in the present moment and realize that this is always where we are.

Being present with your life empowers you to be your best self, and ironically, to authentically be more, do more, and have more without having to stress over it or struggle to get it. All your stress and fears melt away when you are aware of who you truly are at your core. And who you truly are is a beautiful, infinite, dynamic being who is connected to, and one with the joy of All There Is.

Let go of all your false beliefs and embrace your true self. Embrace the power you have in this moment. Stop trying to constantly get somewhere else. Realize that you are already here. Know that the present is where you always are, and that it is here that you have the power to shape your own reality. Never underestimate the power of presence. You are in it all the time; now simply use it to your advantage, consciously and authentically.

Learn to embrace the gift of the present moment and you will learn how to be a conscious participant in your own glorious destiny. Know that you have already arrived to someplace great. Know that:

You Are Here.

About the Author

As an enthusiastic student of life, Dora Nudelman has spent years researching and implementing the key principles for living a happy and fulfilling life. After discovering her own path of purpose and ultimate fulfillment, Dora set out to help others find their own truth and personal brand of passion too. A natural optimist at heart, Dora shares her knowledge with others as a personal-development and self-empowerment writer and author, as well as expert quality of life advisor. Dora is also the founder and owner of The Quality of Life Advisors Group, a company devoted to sharing the key principles for maximizing potential and living a peaceful, proactive, successful, fulfilling, harmonious, and purposeful life. For more information please visit: **www.qualityoflifeadvisors.com**.